Auto Repair for Beginners

A Complete DIY Guide with Step-by-Step Instructions on How to Fix All of Your Car's Most Common Problems for Free at Home

Levy Carlsen

TABLE OF CONTENTS

Preface

Introduction to DIY Auto Repair

In the ever-evolving world of automobiles, there exists a unique subset of individuals who don't just drive their cars but yearn to understand them, maintain them, and often repair them on their own terms. These are the DIY auto repair enthusiasts. If you are holding this book, there's a high likelihood you share this passion, or at least harbor a curiosity towards it.

At the core of **DIY auto repair** lies a multidimensional charm. For many, the idea of rolling up their sleeves, popping the hood, and getting their hands dirty offers a palpable sense of satisfaction. Every time you tighten a bolt, replace a worn-out part, or troubleshoot an unexpected rattle, there's a rewarding feeling of accomplishment. Beyond the sheer joy of hands-on work, there's the confidence gained in understanding the intricate systems and mechanics of what is, for many, their most significant investment after their home.

Financial considerations play an undeniable role in the DIY decision-making process. Every time you undertake a project on your own, you potentially save hundreds, if not thousands of dollars. From the simple oil change to the more complex spark plug replacements, each task completed independently keeps money in your pocket. Over the lifespan of a car, these savings can accumulate to a staggering sum.

But it's essential to establish a foundation before embarking on this journey. Just as you wouldn't set out on a road trip without a map (or at least a reliable GPS), entering the world of auto repair without a fundamental understanding can lead to pitfalls. This is where the balance between technicality and accessibility becomes crucial. While we'll delve deep into the nuts and bolts of car mechanics, it's been a priority to ensure this information remains comprehensible to even those who might not know their alternators from their air filters.

Throughout this book, we'll introduce various **technical terms**, ensuring to provide definitions in layman's terms to maintain clarity without overwhelming newcomers. It's a bridge between the uninitiated and the intricate, drawing a roadmap that gradually transforms the unfamiliar into the understood.

However, as with any hands-on discipline, theory alone isn't enough. While this guide offers a wealth of knowledge, success in DIY auto repair will often come through practice, patience, and persistence. Mistakes are part of the learning curve, but they also bring invaluable lessons.

With that said, it's crucial to set realistic expectations. Not every problem can or should be tackled at home. Recognizing the limits of one's knowledge, skill, and even the workspace and tools available is paramount. Sometimes, seeking professional help isn't just advisable, it's necessary.

In conclusion, the journey of DIY auto repair is as much about the personal growth and understanding one achieves as it is about the practical benefits. It's a world where every challenge faced and every problem solved contributes to a deeper bond with your vehicle and a richer understanding of the marvel of engineering you drive daily. Welcome to this journey, and may the miles ahead be both enlightening and rewarding.

Why This Book Matters

With an abundance of information at our fingertips, the era we live in is often hailed as the age of knowledge. Yet, this same abundance can sometimes be the very source of confusion, especially when navigating the intricacies of a subject as complex and multifaceted as auto repair. From countless online forums to YouTube videos, there is no shortage of advice available. However, the accuracy, reliability, and safety of such information can range from genuinely expert to downright hazardous. It is in this landscape that the importance of a single, comprehensive, and reliable source like this book emerges.

Cars, though common in our daily lives, are intricate marvels of engineering. Understanding their many systems, from the **transmission** to the **exhaust**, requires both breadth and depth of knowledge. While certain platforms might offer in-depth explorations of one topic, they might lack in others, leaving knowledge gaps that can lead to inefficient or even unsafe DIY practices. This is why having a single reference that provides both the forest and the trees becomes indispensable.

For beginners, approaching auto repair can feel daunting. The jargon, the myriad of parts, and the fear of making costly mistakes can deter many. That's where this book's unique approach shines. While maintaining a technical core, we've endeavored to break down concepts in such a way that they become palatable even to those who've never held a wrench. Every **technical term** introduced is not just thrown out but explained, contextualized, and made approachable. In essence, we're not just telling you what to do, but also why and how it matters.

Safety is another paramount concern. Incorrectly approached repairs can not only lead to further vehicle damage but can also pose genuine risks to the individual. In the worst scenarios, improper procedures can result in accidents or injuries. Such pitfalls underscore the need for a guide that doesn't just provide steps, but embeds safety practices within them, making them second nature to the reader.

Furthermore, for those looking to save money through DIY auto repair, it's essential to recognize that improper practices can lead to more significant expenses down the line. A misplaced step or an overlooked detail can turn what should have been a money-saving venture into a costly mistake. Hence, detailed, accurate, and comprehensive advice isn't just about getting the job done; it's about getting the job done right.

While the breadth of this book is vast, covering a wide array of topics, the underlying themes remain consistent: clarity, reliability, safety, and accessibility. It serves as a bridge, connecting you, the reader, to the world of auto repair in a manner that empowers, educates, and instills confidence.

As we transition to our initial chapter, "Setting the Stage for Success", we'll be laying the foundational stones. Ensuring you have the right environment and tools is paramount before diving deeper into specific repair tasks. Just as a chef needs a well-equipped kitchen, so does an aspiring mechanic need a well-prepared workspace. Join us as we guide you in creating the optimal space and toolkit, setting you on the path to becoming an adept home mechanic.

Chapter 1: Setting the Stage for Success

The Importance of Safety

Automobiles, while being our trusted companions on the road, are complex machines comprising thousands of parts, each designed to perform a specific function. When approached without the right understanding and respect, the very vehicle that serves us so loyally can present risks, some severe enough to be life-threatening. This is especially true when we step into the realm of Do-It-Yourself (DIY) auto repair, where the blend of mechanical components, electrical systems, and chemical substances can form a potential hazard.

Understanding and acknowledging the **potential risks** is the first step toward ensuring safety. For instance, a car's weight alone presents a hazard. If not adequately supported when elevated, it can lead to crushing injuries. Similarly, the car battery, though often deemed benign, can be a source of danger. It contains acid and can emit explosive gases. Then there's the myriad of chemicals, like brake fluid, coolant, and transmission fluid, which are harmful if ingested, inhaled, or sometimes even if they come into contact with the skin.

Now, while these facts can sound intimidating, especially to the uninitiated, they're not mentioned to deter, but rather to underline the importance of a methodical and safety-first approach. A little knowledge, combined with the right precautions, can go a long way in ensuring that your DIY journey is both rewarding and secure.

One of the primary tools in your safety arsenal will be **Personal Protective Equipment (PPE)**. Depending on the job at hand, this might include safety glasses to shield your eyes from flying debris or chemicals, gloves to protect your hands from burns or cuts, and respirators to ensure you're not inhaling harmful fumes. Remember, every layer of protection you don can make a world of difference in preventing potential injuries.

Ventilation is another crucial aspect. Many vehicular fluids and substances emit fumes that can be hazardous when inhaled in large amounts or over extended periods. If you're working in a closed space like a garage, ensuring it is well-ventilated can help in dispersing such fumes, making the environment both safer and more comfortable.

Also, always keep a well-stocked **first-aid kit** nearby. Accidents, no matter how minor, are an inherent part of any hands-on work. Whether it's a small cut or a bruise, having the necessary first aid supplies ensures immediate attention, preventing minor injuries from becoming major complications.

Last but not least, never underestimate the importance of knowledge. Familiarize yourself with the task at hand before diving in. Understand not just the steps, but the reasons behind them. The more you know about what you're doing, the more equipped you'll be to anticipate potential issues and handle unforeseen complications.

In conclusion, while the world of DIY auto repair is filled with opportunities to learn, save money, and experience the satisfaction of a job well done, it comes with the imperative to prioritize safety above all else. As the adage goes, "It's better to be safe than sorry." By following the safety measures outlined and always maintaining a vigilant and informed approach, you ensure that your automotive adventures are both successful and safe.

In our next segment, we'll delve into creating an ideal workspace, exploring how the right environment can facilitate smoother operations and further enhance safety. From tools to lighting to the arrangement, every detail plays a role. Join us as we guide you in crafting the perfect setting for your automotive endeavors.

Personal Protective Equipment (PPE)

The world of auto repair, while filled with the prospect of discovery and accomplishment, also demands respect for safety. In this arena, **Personal Protective Equipment (PPE)** stands as the vanguard, shielding DIY enthusiasts from the potential hazards they may encounter. This section meticulously charts out the essential safety gear that you should be familiar with, detailing their significance, and offering pointers on quality brands and sourcing.

1. **Safety Glasses**: These are paramount. Whether you're draining fluids, chipping away rust, or simply inspecting the undercarriage, particles can fly, and chemicals can splash. Safety glasses prevent such debris from reaching your eyes. Brands like **3M** and **DEWALT** offer clear and tinted varieties, ensuring unobstructed vision and protection. Remember, your eyesight is irreplaceable.

2. **Gloves**: The intricate tasks of auto repair demand dexterity, but that doesn't mean your hands should be left vulnerable. From hot surfaces to sharp edges, the threats are myriad. Nitrile gloves are excellent for general tasks, resisting oil and punctures. For heavier work, consider reinforced mechanic gloves. Brands such as **Mechanix Wear** and **Ironclad** provide robust options tailored for automotive tasks.

3. **Respirators**: When sanding or working with chemicals, the air isn't just filled with promise but also with potential respiratory hazards. A good respirator filters out harmful particles, ensuring that your lungs remain uncontaminated. **3M's** range of half and full-face respirators, coupled with their variety of filters, can cater to diverse needs, from paint fumes to dust.

4. **Ear Protection**: While often overlooked, the cacophony of automotive work, especially when employing power tools, can be detrimental to your hearing. Earplugs or earmuffs can dampen these sounds, preserving your auditory health. **Honeywell** and **3M** offer reliable options, ensuring both comfort and efficacy.

5. **Safety Boots**: Dropped tools, spilled fluids, and the mere act of maneuvering around a car demand that your feet be adequately protected. Safety boots with slip-resistant soles and toe protection are vital. Brands like **Red Wing** and **Timberland PRO** meld safety with comfort, ensuring that long hours on your feet don't take an undue toll.

6. **Coveralls or Aprons**: Beyond mere cleanliness, these provide a barrier against chemical spills and hot splashes, preserving both your skin and clothing. Look for options that are both durable and easily washable. Brands such as **Dickies** and **Carhartt** have established their reputation in offering robust workwear tailored for such demands.

7. **Hair and Jewelry Guards**: If you have long hair or wear jewelry, it's imperative to keep them secured and away from moving parts. Simple hairnets or bands can keep your hair in place, and removing jewelry before starting any work can prevent possible entanglements.

Understanding the **why** behind each piece of PPE is as crucial as the act of donning them. Each item is a testament to lessons learned, often the hard way, by countless individuals before us. By equipping yourself adequately, you're not just safeguarding your well-being but ensuring that your DIY journey remains unmarred by avoidable incidents.

As you step further into the world of auto repair, always keep safety at the forefront of your endeavors. Remember, no task is so urgent or essential that it cannot be done safely. And with the right PPE, you're already on the path to ensuring that each project you undertake is not just a success but also a safe one.

Moving forward, we'll delve into the intricacies of crafting the perfect workspace. Just as a painter needs their studio, a DIY auto enthusiast requires a space tailored to their tasks. A space that facilitates efficiency, organization, and, above all, safety. Join us as we guide you through the nuances of setting up the ideal automotive workshop.

Fire Safety in Auto Repair

Fire safety is a subject that might not immediately come to mind when you think of auto repair. Still, considering the array of flammable materials and potential sources of ignition involved in the process, it becomes a paramount concern. The volatile mix of fuels, lubricants, electrical systems, and even friction can sometimes conspire to pose a fire threat. As with many risks, however, proper knowledge and preparation can greatly diminish the danger.

When working on a vehicle, there's a hidden dance of elements: sparks, fuels, and air. Each has its role, and when they converge unintentionally, a fire can ensue. Whether you're a seasoned mechanic or a weekend DIY enthusiast, understanding the fire risks inherent in auto repair is crucial. This section sheds light on these risks, and more importantly, illuminates the path to ensuring you're safeguarded against them.

Fire Extinguishers: One of the most potent allies in your fire safety arsenal is the **fire extinguisher**. This isn't just any generic extinguisher you might find in a kitchen or office setting but one specifically tailored for the challenges of automotive work. Class B extinguishers are designed to tackle flammable liquid fires, making them suitable for gasoline, oil, and grease fires common in auto repair. However, for a more comprehensive solution, consider a Class ABC extinguisher, adept at handling trash, liquid, and electrical fires alike.

Having an extinguisher is one thing; knowing its operation is another. Familiarize yourself with the **PASS** technique:

- **P**ull the pin.

- **A**im the nozzle at the base of the fire.

- **S**queeze the handle.

- **S**weep from side to side.

Regularly inspect your extinguisher for any visible damages or pressure loss and ensure it's within easy reach, yet away from potential fire sources.

Safe Handling of Flammable Materials: Automotive fluids like gasoline, brake fluid, and certain lubricants are inherently flammable. When handling them, use spill-proof containers and funnels. After use, securely cap containers and store them away from direct sunlight and heat sources. Avoid open flames, sparks, or smoking nearby.

Ventilation: A well-ventilated workspace not only disperses harmful fumes but also reduces the concentration of flammable vapors. By ensuring a consistent flow of fresh air, you're safeguarding against the build-up of combustible gases.

Electrical Safety: Faulty wiring or malfunctioning electrical tools can be a hidden fire hazard. Regularly inspect your tools for frayed wires, and always disconnect the vehicle battery when working near fuel systems or carrying out electrical repairs.

Safe Disposal: Rags soaked in oil or other flammable substances can spontaneously combust if left bunched up. Store them in a sealed metal container and dispose of them as hazardous waste.

Being armed with knowledge is the first line of defense against fire hazards in auto repair. By understanding the risks, ensuring your workspace is equipped with the right safety tools, and always prioritizing safe practices, you significantly minimize the chances of a fire-related mishap.

As we progress in our journey, we'll focus on the nuances of tools – your loyal companions in the world of auto repair. Their selection, maintenance, and safe usage are the keystones to ensuring not just efficient but safe automotive work. Join us as we delve deeper into understanding the tools of the trade.

Ventilation and Chemical Handling in Auto Repair

In the intricate ballet of auto repair, where man meets machine, there's a silent partner that's often overlooked – the very air we breathe. The environment within which we work plays a significant role, not just for comfort but, more critically, for safety. Proper **ventilation** ensures that the workspace remains free from hazardous fumes and vapors, while correct chemical handling is the linchpin to ensure that the work environment stays contamination-free. Let's unpack the significance of these aspects.

Breathing Easy: The Role of Ventilation

When you're elbows-deep in an engine bay, replacing an oil filter or adjusting a carburetor, the importance of fresh, clean air might not be immediately evident. Yet, beneath the surface, a myriad of chemicals evaporate, releasing potentially harmful vapors into the air. Gasoline, brake fluid, coolants, and even certain cleaning agents can emit fumes that, in high concentrations, can be harmful or even lethal.

Proper ventilation does more than provide a comfortable working environment; it's a health necessity. An adequately ventilated workspace ensures a constant influx of fresh air, diluting and displacing the hazardous vapors. This is especially crucial when working in enclosed spaces like garages. Whenever possible, work with doors and windows open. For more confined spaces, consider investing in an **extraction fan** or an exhaust system that pulls out stale air, replacing it with fresh air.

Handling with Care: The Chemical Aspect

Automobiles are marvels of engineering, but they also house a cocktail of chemicals, each with its purpose and potential hazards. Understanding these chemicals is fundamental to safe auto repair.

For starters, each chemical or fluid should be stored in its original container, which provides vital information, including its composition, potential hazards, and first-aid measures. In the absence of the original container, label makeshift containers with the chemical's name and potential hazards.

Chemicals like antifreeze, although essential for a vehicle, can be highly toxic if ingested and harmful if they come into contact with the skin. Wearing gloves, protective eyewear, and even aprons can prevent accidental splashes.

Another aspect that often gets sidelined is the safe disposal of chemicals. Draining oil or coolant directly onto the ground or down drains can have lasting environmental consequences. Instead, collect them in sealable containers and dispose of them at local recycling centers or hazardous waste collection sites.

Safe Storage: Keeping Hazards at Bay

The storage of automotive chemicals is equally critical. Flammable substances, like gasoline or brake cleaner, should be stored away from sources of heat or open flames. A well-ventilated, cool, and dry place, preferably a locked cabinet, is ideal for these chemicals. For corrosive chemicals, like certain cleaning agents or battery acid, ensure that they're stored in corrosion-resistant containers and away from materials they can damage.

Navigating the maze of auto repair might seem daunting, especially when considering the chemical aspect. Still, with knowledge as your compass, you're more than equipped to traverse it safely. As we delve deeper into the realms of auto repair, you'll find that understanding and respecting your tools and materials is the key to not only successful repairs but also safe ones. Up next, we'll introduce you to the diverse toolset that will become your trusted allies in this journey.

Setting Up Your Workspace for Efficient and Safe Auto Repair

Your workspace — it's more than just a patch of ground where tasks are carried out. It's the canvas on which the art of auto repair will be etched. Proper setup goes a long way, transforming it from a mere space to an efficient, well-lit, and above all, safe environment. Setting up your workspace is the inaugural step, setting the tone for all the auto-repair tasks that follow. Let's embark on this transformative journey.

Selecting the Right Space

At the heart of any successful DIY auto repair project is the environment within which it's undertaken. Not all spaces are made equal. Your choice can range from a dedicated garage, a driveway, or even a rented workshop space. Regardless of the chosen site, there are three pillars that it must adhere to: it should be spacious, flat, and free from distractions. Maneuvering around a car requires room, especially when dealing with larger parts or when tools like **jacks** and **jack stands** are introduced. A flat surface ensures stability, a critical factor considering the weight and movements involved. Lastly, it's imperative to choose a location where distractions, such as playing children or pets, are minimized.

Illuminating Matters with Proper Lighting

Imagine trying to locate a small bolt dropped inside the engine bay or detecting a tiny crack in a hose. These tasks would be near impossible without the right lighting. Adequate illumination, preferably a mix of **ambient lighting** and focused **task lighting**, can make tasks smoother and safer. Overhead LED lights provide broad coverage, ensuring the workspace is well-lit. For focused tasks, consider using portable LED work lights or even headlamps, allowing you to shine light exactly where needed.

Organization: The Backbone of Efficiency

An organized workspace isn't just pleasing to the eye; it directly impacts the speed, efficiency, and safety of your auto repair tasks. A pegboard with hooks can be an inexpensive solution to keep your tools visible and within arm's reach. Drawer systems, with each drawer dedicated to a particular set of tools, further enhance organization. Labeling these storage spaces might seem overkill but will save you time in the long run.

Next, let's touch upon **mobile tool carts**. These are versatile units that allow you to bring your tools closer to the task at hand, saving repeated trips to the toolbox. Additionally, setting aside dedicated bins or containers for used parts and another for new ones can streamline your workflow.

Safety isn't just about what you wear or the precautions you take but extends to how your workspace is structured. Tripping hazards should be minimized. Electrical cords should be well-managed and kept off walkways, using cord management systems if necessary.

Lastly, consider the future. As your skills and tool collection grow, your workspace might need to evolve. Investing in modular storage solutions now can save time, money, and effort in the future.

In a nutshell, the sanctum of auto repair, your workspace, should be the embodiment of safety, efficiency, and comfort. As we advance in our exploration of DIY auto repair, having a well-set workspace will lay the foundation for success. With your stage set, we'll soon dive into the nuts and bolts – both figuratively and literally – of car maintenance and repair.

Tools and Equipment: The Unsung Heroes of DIY Auto Repair

Behind every successful DIY auto repair is a symphony of tools and equipment. These instruments, ranging from the basic to the specialized, enable both the novice and the seasoned mechanic to carry out tasks with precision, safety, and efficiency. Whether you're just starting on your DIY auto repair journey or looking to refine your tool collection, this section seeks to shed light on the critical tools and equipment that should grace every workspace.

Starting with the Basics

Every toolkit begins with a core set of **hand tools**. These are the unsung heroes of every repair, the tools you'll reach for most frequently. A comprehensive set of wrenches, both standard and metric, is fundamental. Then come the **ratchets and sockets**. They facilitate the turning of bolts in tight spaces where a standard wrench might not fit. Screwdrivers, of various sizes and types (flathead and Phillips), pliers, and an adjustable wrench complete this basic ensemble.

Beyond the Basics: Specialized Tools

As your repair tasks become more intricate, specialized tools might become necessary. Here's where tools like **torque wrenches** come into play, ensuring that bolts are tightened to the precise specifications. If you're delving into tasks that require removal of pulleys or gears, a **puller set** is invaluable. Brake jobs? You'd need a **brake bleeder kit** and a **brake line flare tool**.

Power Tools: Efficiency Multiplied

While hand tools are fantastic for precision, power tools, such as **cordless drills** and **impact wrenches**, magnify your efficiency. They can significantly reduce the time taken for tasks like removing long bolts or drilling. However, remember to always use them with caution. Their torque and speed can be a double-edged sword if not handled correctly.

Lifting and Support: Jacks and Stands

Before you dive beneath a vehicle, ensuring its stability is paramount. **Hydraulic jacks** help lift your car off the ground, but they're not designed to hold the weight for extended periods. Enter **jack stands**, the trusty companions that ensure the car remains elevated safely. Never, and this can't be stressed enough, rely solely on a jack to support a vehicle's weight.

Diagnostic Tools

Sometimes, the challenge isn't the repair itself but identifying the problem. **OBD-II scanners** have democratized diagnostics. By plugging this tool into your car, you can read error codes that provide insights into potential issues. Combined with a **multimeter**, which measures electrical values, these diagnostic tools are gateways to understanding your vehicle's health.

Maintenance and Care for Your Tools

A tool's efficiency isn't just about its quality but also its upkeep. Regularly cleaning your tools, lubricating moving parts, and storing them in dry conditions can greatly extend their lifespan. Investing in a **tool chest** with drawers and separators ensures that every tool has its place, minimizing potential damage.

In the vast world of auto repair, the tools you wield significantly dictate your experience and outcomes. By equipping yourself aptly and understanding the purpose and proper care of each tool, you set the stage for a smoother, safer, and more rewarding DIY journey. As we move forward, these tools will be our constant companions, aiding and guiding us through each repair task.

Essential Hand Tools:

- **Wrenches (Standard and Metric)**: *Craftsman 20-Piece Ratcheting Wrench Set*
  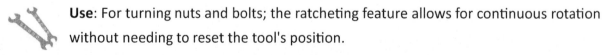 **Use**: For turning nuts and bolts; the ratcheting feature allows for continuous rotation without needing to reset the tool's position.

- **Ratchets and Sockets**: *DeWalt 192-Piece Mechanics Tools Set*
  Use: For tightening and loosening different sizes of fasteners using interchangeable sockets.

- **Screwdrivers**: *Wiha SoftFinish Screwdriver Set*

   Use: For driving or removing screws; comes in various shapes and sizes for different screw heads.

- **Pliers**: *Channellock GS-3 3-Piece Tongue and Groove Plier Set*

   Use: For gripping, bending, and cutting wires or other materials.

- **Adjustable Wrench**: *Stanley 90-947 6-Inch MaxSteel Adjustable Wrench*

   Use: For turning nuts and bolts; the adjustable jaw allows for a range of sizes.

- **Hammer and Mallet**: *Estwing Sure Strike Drilling Hammer*

   Use: For applying force; the mallet typically has a softer head to prevent damage to the surface.

Specialized Hand Tools:

- **Torque Wrenches**: *TEKTON 1/2 Inch Drive Click Torque Wrench*
  Use: For applying a specific torque to a bolt or nut, ensuring it's neither too tight nor too loose.

- **Puller Set**: *OTC 4534 Multipurpose Bearing and Pulley Puller Set*

   Use: For removing gears, pulleys, or bearings from a shaft.

- **Brake Bleeder Kit and Brake Line Flare Tool**: *Mityvac MV6835 Brake Bleeder Kit*

   Use: For removing air bubbles from brake lines and shaping the end of brake lines for a leak-proof connection.

- **Spark Plug Socket**: *GearWrench Magnetic Swivel Spark Plug Set*

   Use: For installing or removing spark plugs in an engine.

- **Oil Filter Wrench**: *Channellock 209 9-Inch Oil Filter & PVC Plier*

   Use: For removing or installing oil filters.

- **Feeler Gauges**: *Lisle 67870 Spark Plug Gauge Gap*

   Use: For measuring small gaps, like the gap between spark plug electrodes.

Power and Air Tools:

- **Cordless Drills and Drill Bits**: *Milwaukee M18 Fuel Drill Driver Kit*

   Use: For drilling holes or driving screws, bolts, and other fasteners.

- **Impact Wrench**: *Ingersoll Rand 2235TiMAX Drive Air Impact Wrench*

   Use: For quickly and powerfully tightening or loosening nuts and bolts.

- **Air Compressor and Pneumatic Tools**: *California Air Tools 8010 Ultra Quiet & Oil-Free*

   Compressor

  Use: Provides compressed air for various tools, like impact wrenches, nail guns, and paint sprayers.

Lifting and Support Equipment:

- **Hydraulic Jacks**: *Arcan 3-Ton Quick Rise Aluminum Floor Jack*

   Use: For lifting vehicles or other heavy objects off the ground.

- **Jack Stands**: *ESCO 10498 Jack Stand, 3-Ton Capacity*

   Use: For safely supporting a lifted vehicle.

- **Wheel Chocks**: *MaxxHaul Tandem Wheel Chock/Lock*

   Use: To prevent vehicles from rolling while working on them.

Diagnostic and Electrical Tools:

- **OBD-II Scanners**: *Autel AutoLink AL319 OBD2 Scanner*

   Use: For reading vehicle diagnostic codes from the onboard computer.

- **Multimeter**: *Fluke 117 Electricians True RMS Multimeter*

  Use: For measuring electrical properties like voltage, current, and resistance.

- **Test Light**: *Innova 3420 Smart Test Light/Circuit Tester*

  Use: For checking the presence of electrical current in a circuit.

- **Battery Charger and Jump Starter**: *NOCO Genius10 Fully-Automatic Smart Charger*

  Use: For charging vehicle batteries or providing a boost to start a dead battery.

Organization and Storage:

- **Tool Chest**: *Husky 9-Drawer Deep Tool Chest Mobile Workbench*
   Use: For organizing and storing tools.

- **Parts Trays and Magnetic Bowls**: *Titan Tools Mini Magnetic Parts Tray*
   **Use**: For holding and organizing small parts, screws, nuts, and bolts.

- **Pegboards**: *Wall Control Galvanized Steel Pegboard Pack*
   **Use**: For hanging and organizing tools on walls.

Additional Essentials:

- **Creeper**: *Pro-LifT C-9100 Black 40" Foldable Z Creeper*
   Use: For easily moving around underneath a vehicle while working.

- **Work Gloves**: *Mechanix Wear - Original Work Gloves*
   Use: For hand protection during mechanical work.

- **Flashlight or Work Light**: *Astro Pneumatic Tool 40SLMAX 450 Lumen Rechargeable LED Slim Light* **Use**: For illuminating dark or hard-to-see areas.

- **Mechanic's Stethoscope**: *Lisle 52500 Mechanic's Stethoscope*
  Use: For listening to specific sounds in an engine to diagnose issues.

- **Pry Bars**: *GearWrench 82301 3 Piece Pry Bar Set*
  Use: For leveraging or separating components.

These recommendations are based on brand reputation and known quality as of 2021. It's always wise to check updated reviews and research newer models when shopping for tools.

Organizing Your Garage or Workspace

When you embark on the journey of DIY auto repair, the environment in which you work plays a significant role in determining both your efficiency and safety. Picture this: a cluttered garage where you're constantly tripping over tools, searching endlessly for that one wrench you need, or losing tiny but essential parts amidst the chaos. Not exactly the ideal scenario, right? Hence, before you delve into the nitty-gritty of auto mechanics, it's pivotal to optimize your workspace. Here's how.

Space Designation: Start by designating specific zones in your garage or workspace. A **zone system** means allocating specific areas for specific tasks. For example, a workbench zone for intricate tasks, a vehicle zone where you actually work on your car, and storage zones for your tools and supplies. By having a designated spot for each activity, you streamline your workflow and reduce the chances of mishaps.

Invest in Quality Storage: The saying "a place for everything and everything in its place" couldn't be truer here. Good storage doesn't just mean a clutter-free space; it means quicker access, fewer lost items, and a safer environment. Consider getting a **tool chest** or a cabinet system. These come in various sizes and configurations and provide a centralized location for your tools. Magnetic strips can be ideal for holding your frequently used tools, while pegboards are versatile for hanging items of various sizes. Don't overlook the importance of small bins and containers for nuts, bolts, and other minuscule parts. Label everything; it might seem like a tedious task now, but it will save you heaps of time in the long run.

Safety First: An organized workspace is a safe workspace. By ensuring there's no clutter on the floor, you're minimizing tripping hazards. Moreover, designate a secure spot for flammable materials and make sure they're away from any potential ignition sources. Remember, accidents often occur when we least expect them, but a well-organized space minimizes these unexpected risks.

Optimize Lighting: A well-lit space doesn't just make tasks easier; it also reduces the risk of mistakes. Ensure you have a mix of general overhead lighting and task-specific lighting. Portable and adjustable work lights can be a godsend when working under the car or in dimly lit areas.

Workflow Matters: Think about the natural progression of tasks when organizing. You wouldn't want to store your wrenches far away from where you're likely to use them, would you? Set up your workspace in a way that allows you to move seamlessly from one task to another. This involves not only organizing tools logically but also setting up your vehicle zone efficiently. If you have the luxury of space, consider investing in a **creeper**, which allows for easier and more comfortable access under your vehicle.

By now, you should have a fair idea of how to transform your garage or workspace into a haven of productivity and safety. It might require some investment of time, effort, and perhaps even money, but remember: the dividends it pays in terms of time saved, frustrations avoided, and potential accidents averted make it all worthwhile.

As we conclude this foundational chapter, remember that a conducive workspace is the backbone of any successful DIY auto repair endeavor. But a well-organized space alone isn't enough. To truly excel, you'll need a deep understanding of the vehicle you're working on. Which brings us to our next chapter: **Understanding Your Vehicle**. Dive deep into the complex, yet fascinating world of automobile mechanics, dissecting systems and components, and empowering you with the knowledge you need to tackle any DIY challenge head-on. Join us, and let's embark on this enlightening journey together.

Chapter 2: Understanding Your Vehicle

Reading and Understanding the Owner's Manual

In the age of digital search engines and online forums, one might wonder about the relevance of an old-school document like an **owner's manual**. Is it just an archaic booklet that you toss into the glove compartment and forget? Absolutely not. The owner's manual serves as the unsung hero for DIY car enthusiasts and is an invaluable tool to understand the intricate details and secrets your vehicle holds.

When you buy a new electronic gadget, say a smartphone or a laptop, you're excited to explore its features. But without an understanding of its functions, you might only scratch the surface of its capabilities. Similarly, the owner's manual of your car is its 'user guide'. It details how to use, maintain, and troubleshoot your vehicle, ensuring you get the most out of its performance while staying safe.

So, why is this booklet so crucial? The answer is simple: personalization. Every car model is unique. While general mechanical principles remain the same, manufacturers often have specific recommendations or features designed for their vehicles. The owner's manual is your key to these nuances.

Inside this treasure trove, you'll find a plethora of information:

1. **Specifications:** From engine size to tire pressure, the manual will provide you with the specific details of your vehicle. It's essential to adhere to these, especially when replacing parts or fluids, to ensure longevity and optimal performance.

2. **Maintenance Schedule:** Wondering when to change the oil, replace the air filter, or check the brakes? The manual provides a timeline, generally based on mileage, to keep your car in peak condition. By following this schedule, you're not just ensuring smooth rides but also potentially saving on future repair costs.

3. **Warning Lights and Indicators:** The myriad of lights on your dashboard isn't just for show. Each symbol, whether it's a check engine light or a tire pressure warning, communicates vital information about your car's health. Your manual will decode these symbols, guiding you on the appropriate steps to take.

4. **Safety Precautions:** This section is crucial, especially for those new to DIY auto repairs. The manual will point out areas or components that might be hazardous if not handled correctly.

5. **Troubleshooting:** Before you panic over a weird noise or a malfunctioning component, consult the manual. Often, it will have a troubleshooting section that can guide you through common problems and their potential solutions.

Now, the challenge for many is the perceived complexity of the document. However, manufacturers design these manuals with the user in mind. They're typically organized into sections, with a table of contents upfront and an index at the back. For a quick answer, the index is your best friend. Need to know about the battery? Look it up in the index, and it'll direct you to the relevant page.

As we delve further into understanding your vehicle, always remember that the owner's manual is your primary compass. It's your vehicle's voice, offering insights and advice tailored for your specific make and model. While it might not answer every question, especially when we move into advanced repairs and modifications, it's the foundation upon which your DIY auto repair journey should be built.

With the foundational knowledge of the owner's manual under our belt, we're poised to delve deeper into the mechanical world of our vehicles. As we progress through this chapter, we'll uncover more layers of our automotive companions, ensuring that by the end, you'll view your car not just as a mode of transport but as a marvel of engineering awaiting your expert touch.

Identifying and Understanding Basic Car Components

In our journey through the automotive world, understanding the key components of a vehicle is paramount. Picture your car as a puzzle, each piece playing a role in the bigger picture. Today, we'll delve deeper into each major system, breaking them down into their primary components, each described for clarity.

1. **Engine**

   - **Cylinders**: Hollow chambers where fuel is burned to produce power. Their count (e.g., four, six, eight) often defines the engine type.

   - **Pistons**: Metal plugs that move up and down inside the cylinders, converting fuel combustion into mechanical movement.

   - **Crankshaft**: A long metal bar connected to the pistons, converting their up-and-down motion into a rotational movement to drive the wheels.

   - **Camshaft**: Regulates the opening and closing of intake and exhaust valves, ensuring the right amount of air-fuel mixture enters and exits the cylinders.

   - **Timing Belt/Chain**: Ensures the synchronized operation of the camshaft and crankshaft.

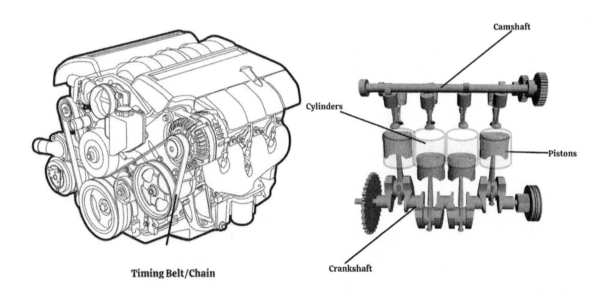

2. **Transmission**

- **Clutch**: Engages and disengages power flow between the engine and transmission, essential for manual transmissions.

- **Gearbox**: Contains a set of gears that can be adjusted to control speed and torque.

- **Drive Shaft**: Transmits the rotational power from the transmission to the wheels.

- **Differential**: Distributes engine power to the wheels, allowing them to rotate at different speeds, especially in turns.

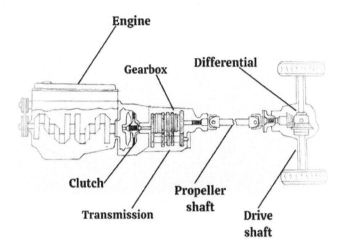

3. **Exhaust System**

- **Exhaust Manifold**: Collects exhaust gases from multiple cylinders into one pipe.

- **Catalytic Converter**: Transforms harmful pollutants into less harmful emissions.

- **Muffler**: Reduces noise from the exhaust process.

- **Tailpipe**: The endpoint where the cleaned and muffled exhaust gases are released.

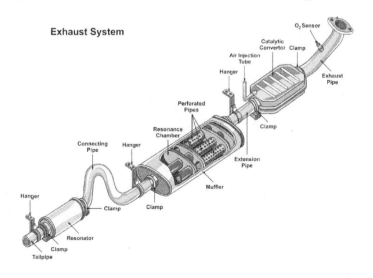

4. Cooling System

- **Radiator**: Helps in cooling the hot coolant coming from the engine.

- **Thermostat**: Regulates the flow of coolant based on the engine's temperature.

- **Water Pump**: Circulates coolant between the engine and the radiator.

- **Cooling Fans**: Aid in reducing the temperature of the coolant in the radiator.

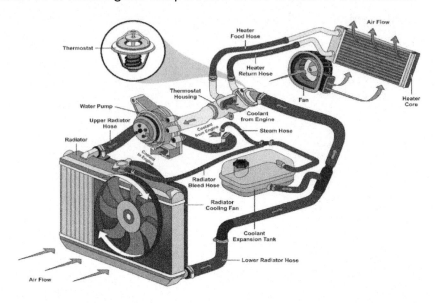

5. Electrical System

- **Battery**: Stores and provides electrical energy.

- **Alternator**: Generates electrical power while the engine is running and charges the battery.

- **Starter Motor**: Uses electricity from the battery to start the engine.

- **Spark Plugs**: Ignites the air-fuel mixture in the cylinders.

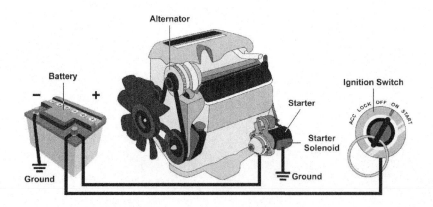

6. **Brake System**

- **Brake Pads/Shoes**: Creates friction to slow down or stop the vehicle.

- **Rotors/Drums**: Paired with pads or shoes to produce the necessary friction.

- **Brake Lines**: Transfers brake fluid under pressure from the master cylinder to the brakes.

- **Master Cylinder**: The primary reservoir for brake fluid, which is pressurized when applying brakes.

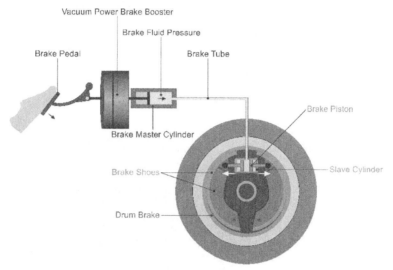

7. **Suspension System**

- **Springs**: Absorb shocks from the road.

- **Shock Absorbers**: Dissipate the energy absorbed by springs.

- **Control Arms**: Connect the vehicle's framework to the steering knuckles.

- **Ball Joints**: Allow for rotational movement between the control arms and steering knuckles.

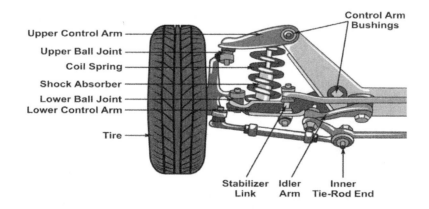

8. **Fuel System**

- **Fuel Tank**: Stores the vehicle's fuel.

- **Fuel Pump**: Delivers fuel from the tank to the engine.

- **Fuel Filters**: Ensures that the fuel going into the engine is free from contaminants.

- **Fuel Injectors**: Spray the right amount of fuel into the engine for combustion.

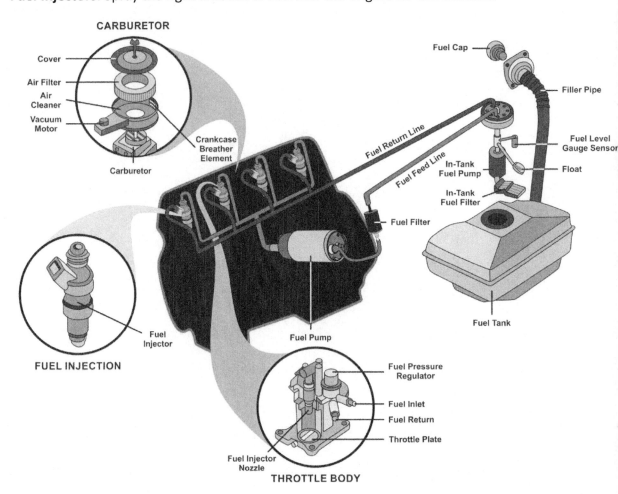

9. **Steering System**

   - **Steering Wheel**: Allows the driver to control the direction of the vehicle.

   - **Steering Column**: Connects the steering wheel to the steering mechanism.

   - **Rack and Pinion**: Converts the rotational movement of the steering wheel into the left or right motion of the wheels.

   - **Power Steering Pump**: Assists in making steering easier by using hydraulic pressure.

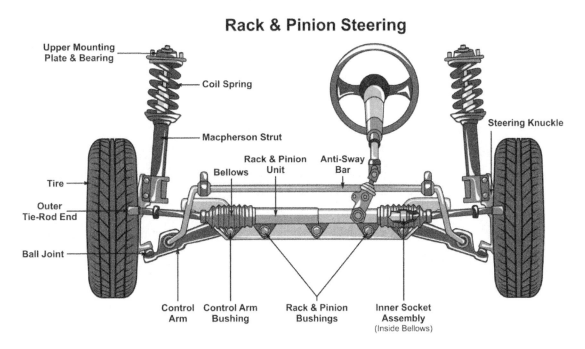

Rack & Pinion Steering

As you can now see, each major system of a car is a complex assembly of interrelated components. Having this foundational understanding is crucial as we progress, giving context to every repair or maintenance task we encounter. While these descriptions give a broad overview, remember that there's a depth of intricacies to explore in each component. As we dive deeper into automotive specifics, you'll be equipped to see not just a puzzle but the masterpiece it forms.

Vehicle Maintenance Schedules

As we delve deeper into understanding our vehicles, the **vehicle maintenance schedule** stands out as an integral component. This document, often overshadowed by other sections in the owner's manual, is your car's strategic plan for health and longevity. It is the distillation of extensive research and expertise from the vehicle's designers and engineers.

Every vehicle is akin to a finely-tuned orchestra, where each instrument or part has its rhythm and timeline. The maintenance schedule is the maestro that ensures each component functions harmoniously over time. It systematically lists out intervals for inspection, servicing, and replacement of parts based on the vehicle's age, mileage, or both.

To locate this treasure trove of information, turn to your vehicle's owner's manual. While it might initially seem daunting given its dense content, it's organized methodically. Usually, sections titled 'Maintenance', 'Service Intervals', or 'Routine Care' are where you'd find the maintenance chart. These charts, typically in tabular form, detail activities against specific milestones, be it mileage like 10,000 miles, 20,000 miles, or timeframes like 6 months, 12 months, etc.

Interpreting the maintenance schedule is crucial. These charts are filled with a combination of intervals and recommended actions. For instance:

- **Oil Changes:** Often recommended every 5,000 to 7,500 miles. Over time, engine oil can break down, losing its viscosity and lubricating properties. Regular changes ensure the engine remains lubricated, reducing wear.

- **Air Filters:** Replacement might be suggested around the 15,000 to 30,000-mile mark. Air filters ensure only clean air enters the engine, enhancing efficiency. A clogged filter can hamper performance and fuel efficiency.

- **Brake Inspections:** Usually around every 10,000 miles. Brakes are vital for safety, and regular checks ensure they function optimally, detecting issues like worn pads or low brake fluid.

- **Battery Checks:** Typically, every 20,000 miles or annually. Batteries power various vehicle components, and ensuring their health can prevent unexpected breakdowns.

- **Tire Rotations and Checks:** Every 6,000 to 8,000 miles. This ensures even tire wear, extending their life and ensuring safe and efficient performance.

- **Coolant Replacement:** Around 60,000 miles or every 4 years. Coolant keeps the engine from overheating, and regular replacement ensures it remains effective.

Heeding this schedule is non-negotiable. While one might be tempted to delay maintenance citing various reasons, doing so can have detrimental effects. Delayed maintenance doesn't just reduce efficiency; it can accelerate wear and tear, leading to expensive repairs. Moreover, it can jeopardize safety.

Maintaining a vehicle goes beyond ensuring a smooth drive. It's about guaranteeing reliability, optimizing performance, and safeguarding investments. Regular maintenance isn't an expense; it's an investment into the longevity and health of your vehicle.

As we cap off this chapter, it becomes clear that understanding a vehicle is holistic. It's not just about parts but about nurturing a relationship with your vehicle, ensuring its well-being. The next journey on our exploration takes us right into the heart and soul of our vehicles. **Chapter 3: Understanding Engines and Fuel Types** will unpack the different engines' intricacies and the fuels that keep them running. Get ready to unravel the marvels beneath the hood!

Chapter 3: Understanding Engines and Fuel Types

How Gasoline Engines Work

If cars are the symphony of modern mobility, then the engine is the lead maestro that orchestrates its harmonious movement. Delving into the world of gasoline engines is like uncovering a beautifully choreographed ballet of mechanical parts, and we'll journey through this dance, step by step.

At the heart of our vehicles is the **internal combustion engine**. The term might sound daunting, but let's break it down. As the name implies, "internal combustion" simply means that fuel is burned (or combusted) inside the engine in small, confined spaces called **combustion chambers**. This burning process releases energy, pushing the **pistons** inside the engine, leading to the vehicle's movement.

Imagine a bicycle pump. When you push down, the air is compressed and forced out. Similarly, in a gasoline engine, the piston moves up, compressing the air and fuel mixture. When it's ignited by the **spark plug**, it expands violently, pushing the piston down and turning the **crankshaft**. This rotation is what ultimately drives the car's wheels.

Now, the process I've just described, in engine-speak, is known as a **stroke**. A gasoline engine typically operates on a four-stroke cycle: Intake, Compression, Combustion (or Power), and Exhaust.

1. **Intake:** During the intake stroke, the piston moves down, and an air-fuel mixture enters the combustion chamber through the open **intake valve**. Think of this as the engine taking a deep breath in preparation for a vigorous activity.

2. **Compression:** With the intake valve closed, the piston moves up, compressing the air-fuel mixture. This is akin to you squishing a spring in your hand, building up potential energy.

3. **Combustion (Power):** The spark plug ignites the compressed mixture. The resulting explosion forces the piston down with great power. This single step is where the actual energy to move the car is produced.

4. **Exhaust:** After the power stroke, the **exhaust valve** opens, allowing the piston to push out the burned gases, clearing the chamber for the next intake of fresh air and fuel.

This entire process happens remarkably fast, with engines executing thousands of these cycles every minute. The dance of the pistons, the opening, and closing of valves, and the spark from the spark plug are all meticulously timed to perfection.

An engine isn't just about power, though. Efficiency, smoothness, and reliability are all crucial. That's why we have other vital components. The **oil pump** circulates engine oil to keep parts lubricated, the **water pump** and **radiator** keep the engine at the optimal temperature, and the **fuel pump** ensures that the right amount of gasoline is always available.

Fuel, in this context, is of paramount importance. Gasoline engines are designed to work best with specific types of gasoline. The **octane rating** of gasoline is a measure of its resistance to knocking or pinging during combustion. Using the correct octane fuel is essential for your engine's longevity and efficiency.

In essence, the gasoline engine is a marvelous piece of engineering, converting liquid fuel into kinetic energy, propelling our vehicles forward. Understanding this intricate system puts you a step closer to appreciating the genius behind modern mobility.

As we close this chapter, it's evident how vital engines are in our daily commute. However, the gasoline engine is just one type in the vast spectrum of engines available. Our journey into the world of mobility is far from over. As we transition into our next topic, we will delve deeper into the realm of different fuel types and how each contributes to the automotive symphony. Stay tuned for an enlightening ride!

How Diesel Engines Work

Having embarked on the rhythmic journey of gasoline engines, we now steer our exploration towards the robust and efficient world of **diesel engines**. They share many similarities with their gasoline counterparts, but the unique characteristics of diesel fuel and the engine's operation make them distinct and fascinating.

At its core, a diesel engine is also an **internal combustion engine**. This means that it burns fuel inside the engine to produce power, much like gasoline engines. However, the method it employs to ignite the fuel is notably different, and this is where our story begins.

While gasoline engines use spark plugs to ignite an air-fuel mixture, diesel engines utilize the concept of **compression ignition**. In simpler terms, the air inside the combustion chamber is compressed so much that its temperature rises dramatically. When diesel fuel is then injected into this super-hot, highly compressed air, it ignites spontaneously. No spark required!

The step-by-step process of a diesel engine is comparable to the four-stroke cycle we covered with gasoline engines, but with key distinctions:

1. **Intake:** Only air is drawn into the combustion chamber, unlike gasoline engines which take in an air-fuel mixture. The diesel engine's deep inhalation fills the chamber with fresh air.

2. **Compression:** As the piston rises, the air is compressed to a much higher degree than in gasoline engines. This compression generates intense heat, raising the air's temperature above the diesel fuel's ignition point.

3. **Combustion (Power):** At the pinnacle of compression, diesel fuel is sprayed into the chamber through **fuel injectors**. The sheer heat of the compressed air causes the diesel to ignite, forcing the piston down and producing power. This method of ignition gives diesel engines their trademark efficiency and torque.

4. **Exhaust:** Post combustion, the burned gases are expelled out, resetting the chamber for the next cycle.

One might wonder about the advantages of such a process. Diesel engines, due to their higher compression, are often more efficient than gasoline engines. They deliver better fuel economy and produce more torque, making them a favorite for heavy-duty vehicles like trucks and buses.

However, the benefits don't stop at efficiency. Diesel fuel has a higher **energy density** than gasoline, meaning it contains more potential energy per liter. This is one reason why diesel engines often get better mileage than their gasoline counterparts.

But it's not all sunshine and rainbows. Diesel engines historically had a reputation for being noisier, emitting more pollutants, and being less refined than gasoline engines. Modern technology, however, has come a long way. Advances in **turbocharging**, **after-treatment systems**, and more precise fuel injection have made today's diesel engines quieter, cleaner, and more pleasant to drive.

When comparing diesel and gasoline engines, it's essential to remember they're designed for different tasks. While gasoline engines often prioritize quick acceleration and high-speed performance, diesel engines focus on efficiency and pulling power.

To round off our exploration of diesel engines, it's worth noting their vast contributions to the transport and industrial sectors. Their unmatched efficiency and durability make them indispensable in many applications.

We've now voyaged through the realms of both gasoline and diesel engines, each with its unique symphony of power and efficiency. As our journey advances, we'll delve into other fuel types and engine technologies, further enriching our understanding of the vast automotive landscape. Join us as we shift gears into our next segment, unveiling the intricacies of alternative fuel sources. The road ahead promises to be both enlightening and exhilarating!

How Hybrid Engines Work

Continuing our expedition through the dynamic world of engines, we now arrive at a fascinating crossroads of innovation and sustainability - the **hybrid engine**. With the climate crisis and soaring fuel prices, it's no surprise that hybrid technology has been at the forefront of automotive advancements. But what exactly makes these engines "hybrid", and how do they seamlessly blend electric and gasoline propulsion?

A hybrid vehicle combines two power sources: an **internal combustion engine** (typically gasoline-powered) and an **electric motor**. Think of it as having the best of both worlds: the extended range and familiar refueling process of a gasoline engine, coupled with the quiet, efficient operation of an electric motor.

At its heart, the primary advantage of a hybrid system is its ability to optimize efficiency based on driving conditions. Let's break down the harmonious dance between these two power sources:

1. **Starting and Low Speeds:** Often, when you start a hybrid vehicle or drive at slow speeds, only the electric motor is at work. This is highly efficient as electric motors consume no fuel and produce zero emissions during these conditions.

2. **Acceleration and High Demand:** When rapid acceleration is required, or when the vehicle is under a significant load (like driving uphill), both the gasoline engine and the electric motor work together. The combined power of both units offers swift acceleration while maintaining a decent level of fuel efficiency.

3. **Cruising:** At steady speeds on highways, the gasoline engine typically takes over. The electric motor might occasionally pitch in to provide a boost or save fuel, depending on the driving conditions and battery charge level.

4. **Braking:** Hybrid vehicles use a technology called **regenerative braking**. Rather than wasting the energy produced during braking, it's captured and used to recharge the onboard batteries that power the electric motor. It's a fantastic way to recover and reuse energy that would otherwise be lost.

5. **Resting & Stops:** At traffic lights or during short stops, the gasoline engine might turn off completely, saving fuel. The electric system manages essential functions, like air conditioning and radio, ensuring the cabin remains comfortable.

The heart of a hybrid system lies in its **battery pack**. Unlike the small battery in conventional vehicles, a hybrid's battery is sophisticated, capable of storing and releasing energy for the electric motor. This battery gets its energy from two sources: the aforementioned regenerative braking and the gasoline engine, which acts as a generator during certain operating conditions.

One might ponder, "Why not just go fully electric?". Well, while electric vehicles (EVs) are a promising future, current challenges like limited range, long charging times, and a lack of widespread charging infrastructure make hybrids a perfect middle-ground. They bridge the gap between traditional gasoline-powered vehicles and EVs, offering a taste of electrification without the associated range anxiety.

In wrapping up our discussion on hybrid engines, it's essential to acknowledge the broader environmental implications. While hybrids do emit greenhouse gases from their gasoline engines, their overall emissions are generally lower than traditional vehicles, especially in city driving scenarios. By adopting such technologies, we inch closer to a sustainable, eco-friendly future in automotive transport.

Now, having explored the gasoline, diesel, and hybrid realms, our next avenue delves deeper into the heart of pure electrification. Buckle up as we journey through the intricacies of fully electric engines, unlocking the future's potential!

The Main Differences Between Gasoline, Diesel, and Hybrid Engines

As you embark on the enlightening journey of understanding your vehicle better, one of the essential areas to focus on is the beating heart of any automobile - the engine. While all engines share the core goal of converting fuel into movement, the way they achieve this differs significantly based on their type. Gasoline, diesel, and hybrid engines stand out as three distinct choices in today's market. So, how do they differ, and which might be the best fit for you? Let's delve into these engines' unique characteristics.

Efficiency: The term "efficiency" refers to how well an engine can convert fuel into usable energy. **Gasoline engines** are commonly used in most cars due to their lightweight nature and smooth operation. However, when it comes to raw fuel efficiency, **diesel engines** often have the upper hand. They operate at higher compression ratios, extracting more energy from every drop of fuel. On the other hand, **hybrid engines** aim to optimize efficiency by merging the strengths of electric motors with those of internal combustion engines. Especially in stop-and-go city traffic, hybrids can save a considerable amount of fuel.

Emissions: From an environmental perspective, emissions are a hot topic. Gasoline engines tend to emit less of the particulate matter and nitrogen oxides that diesels are often criticized for. However, diesels often produce less carbon dioxide, a primary greenhouse gas. **Hybrids**, with their partial reliance on electricity, often lead the pack in lower emissions, particularly during city drives where the electric motor is frequently in use.

Performance: When it comes to sheer power and acceleration, each engine has its strengths. Gasoline engines provide quick acceleration, making them fun for zippy city drives. Diesels, with their impressive torque, shine in scenarios requiring power, like towing. Hybrids offer a balanced performance, with the electric motor delivering instant torque and the gasoline engine contributing to higher speeds.

Cost of Ownership: Over the long haul, the cost of owning a vehicle isn't just about its sticker price. Gasoline is generally cheaper than diesel, but diesel engines are often more fuel-efficient. So, it becomes a balancing act. Maintenance for diesel engines can be costlier due to their complex turbochargers and exhaust after-treatment systems. Hybrid vehicles introduce another variable: the battery. While they save on fuel costs, battery replacement (after several years) can be an expense to consider.

Other Key Factors: Diesel engines are renowned for their durability and long lifespan, often outlasting their gasoline counterparts. However, with the evolving landscape of emission regulations, diesel's place in the urban setting is often questioned. Hybrids, while sophisticated, demand an understanding of their dual systems and can be a learning curve for drivers transitioning from traditional setups.

As vehicles evolve and the automotive landscape changes, the choice between gasoline, diesel, and hybrid will depend on individual needs and preferences. It's crucial to weigh the pros and cons, keeping in mind your driving patterns, budget, and environmental concerns.

In the chapters to come, we will further equip you with knowledge and tools to be an informed vehicle owner. Next, we shift gears from understanding the heart of your vehicle to the hands-on aspect of car ownership. **Chapter 4: Basic Maintenance Skills** promises to be an empowering guide, offering insights into simple yet essential tasks to keep your vehicle in tip-top shape. From oil checks to tire rotations, we'll demystify the basic rituals that can save you time, money, and ensure your vehicle's longevity.

Chapter 4: Basic Maintenance Skills

Changing Engine Oil and Filter

The heart of your vehicle, the engine, requires regular maintenance to ensure its longevity and efficiency. One of the most fundamental and crucial procedures that every car owner should be familiar with is changing the engine oil and its accompanying filter. Think of the oil as your engine's lifeblood. It ensures everything runs smoothly, minimizes wear and tear, and keeps the engine cool. But why change it? And how often? Let's delve deeper.

Over time, as your engine operates, tiny metal shavings, dirt, and other contaminants make their way into the engine oil. These impurities can cause wear on your engine's delicate components. The oil filter catches many of these contaminants, but even the filter has a limit to its effectiveness. When oil becomes too dirty, and the filter becomes clogged, they no longer function optimally, leading to reduced engine efficiency and potential damage. Hence, regular oil and filter changes are paramount.

Now, let's walk you through the process. Remember, always refer to your owner's manual for specific guidelines related to your vehicle, but here's a general overview:

1. **Preparation:** Proper groundwork ensures a smoother process. Start by collating all the tools and supplies required:

- **Engine Oil:** Check your vehicle's manual to identify the right grade and quantity of oil suited for your engine. Remember, not all engine oils are created equal; using the wrong one can lead to decreased efficiency or even damage.

- **Oil Filter:** Again, refer to your manual or consult with a parts store to get the appropriate filter. Different engines have different requirements, and using an unsuitable filter can be counterproductive.

- **Oil Catch Pan:** This will catch the old oil as it drains. Ensure it's large enough to hold the amount of oil your vehicle holds.

- **Oil Filter Wrench:** This tool aids in removing the old oil filter. There are several types available, so pick one that fits your filter.

- **Socket Set:** Essential for removing and replacing the oil drain plug.

- **Funnel:** To prevent spills when pouring the new oil.

- **Gloves and Safety Goggles:** Safety first! Protect your hands from hot oil and your eyes from unexpected splashes.

- **Rags or Paper Towels:** For cleanup.

- **Jack and Jack Stands (if necessary):** If your vehicle sits low, you might need these to access the drain plug and filter.

2. **Draining Old Oil:** Start with a slightly warm engine – it ensures the oil flows out smoothly. Position the catch pan beneath the **oil drain plug**. Using the appropriate socket or spanner, carefully remove the plug, allowing the old oil to drain out into the pan. Exercise caution as the oil might be hot.

3. **Changing the Oil Filter:** Nearby, you'll locate the oil filter. Using the oil filter wrench, unscrew the old filter. A bit of oil will likely come out, so have the catch pan ready. Before installing the new filter, lightly coat the rubber gasket on its top with some new oil. This ensures a tight seal. Screw the new filter in place by hand until snug.

4. **Refilling with Fresh Oil:** With the drain plug replaced and tightened, it's time to pour in the new oil. Using a funnel, carefully pour the new engine oil into the **oil filler cap** on top of the engine. Don't overfill; always check the amount recommended in your manual.

5. **Checking the Oil Level:** After adding the recommended quantity of oil, pull out the **dipstick**, wipe it clean, reinsert it, then pull it out again to check the oil level. It should be between the two marks. If it's lower, add more oil gradually until it reaches the correct level.

6. **Disposing of Used Oil:** Lastly, and crucially, never dump old oil down drains or in the trash. It's environmentally hazardous. Instead, transfer it to containers and take it to a recycling center or auto shop that disposes of old oil.

Common mistakes to avoid include over-tightening the drain plug or filter, which can strip the threads, and neglecting to replace the oil filter. Changing the oil but leaving a dirty filter counteracts the benefit of fresh oil.

While the procedure might sound a tad technical, once you've done it a couple of times, it becomes second nature. Regularly changing your engine oil and filter ensures your car serves you reliably for miles to come.

Having grasped the essence of oil and filter change, our next chapter will usher you into other realms of basic maintenance. Knowing your vehicle isn't just about understanding its anatomy, but also about being hands-on in its care. Stay tuned as we embark on more enlightening paths, ensuring you're not just driving your vehicle but also nurturing it.

Disposing of Used Oil Properly

In the journey of vehicle ownership, maintenance tasks like oil changes are as routine as refueling. However, after extracting the old engine oil, one is left with the perplexing question: "What do I do with this now?" The answer isn't simply tossing it in the trash or pouring it down a drain; such acts are not only environmentally detrimental but also legally punishable in many jurisdictions. Instead, used motor oil must be treated with the reverence it deserves, ensuring its disposal neither harms our delicate ecosystem nor attracts legal consequences.

Understanding the environmental implications sets the stage for appreciating responsible disposal. When improperly discarded, used engine oil can contaminate soil, groundwater, rivers, and oceans. Even a single liter can sully vast amounts of freshwater. This contamination poses severe risks to aquatic life, plants, and even human health. This isn't just an eco-friendly perspective; it's an essential paradigm for preserving our planet and its resources.

But what's the fuss about used engine oil? The oil from your engine, over time, accumulates **heavy metals**, **chemicals**, and other **contaminants**. These substances can be toxic to the environment. Imagine the chain of events: oil leaks into the soil, is carried into water sources, infiltrates our food chain, and eventually comes back to haunt us and other living beings. Recognizing this cycle accentuates the necessity of proper disposal.

So, how do you go about it? Here's a roadmap:

1. **Containment:** Once you've drained the oil, transfer it to a leak-proof container. Many people use the empty containers from the new oil they've just added to their car. Ensure the container's cap is secured tightly, avoiding any spills during transportation.

2. **Avoid Mixing:** It's crucial to store only motor oil in the container. Even a small inclusion of other fluids, like antifreeze or solvents, can render the entire batch unrecyclable. This is due to the distinct refining processes required for various fluids.

3. **Locate a Collection Site:** Many auto parts stores and service stations act as collection points for used motor oil. Some municipalities also have designated drop-off locations or organize periodic collection events. Websites and hotlines are available to aid in locating your nearest facility.

4. **Understanding Regulations:** The regulatory landscape for used oil disposal varies between regions. Some places may have stringent laws with hefty fines for inappropriate disposal. Familiarizing yourself with local **ordinances** and regulations ensures you're both eco-conscious and law-abiding.

5. **Recycling Oil Filters:** An often-overlooked facet is the oil filter. These filters also accumulate contaminants over time. Many collection sites accept used oil filters alongside the oil. Ensure you drain them thoroughly before disposal.

Embracing proper disposal procedures not only reflects environmental stewardship but can also save you from potential legal penalties. In some regions, the improper disposal of motor oil is met with sizable fines, community service, or even imprisonment, depending on the magnitude of the infringement.

In essence, proper disposal of used motor oil isn't merely an act of eco-kindness; it's a civic responsibility and a legal mandate. By taking these steps, you're playing a part in preserving the environment for future generations and ensuring that our shared resources remain uncontaminated.

As we journey deeper into the realm of car maintenance, our next chapter will focus on providing you with vital insights and hands-on guidance to ensure your vehicle remains in prime condition. Join us as we delve further, equipping you with the knowledge to be not just a car owner but a responsible steward of both your vehicle and the environment.

Replacing Air Filters

The heart of every vehicle, the engine, requires clean air to function optimally. Just as our lungs need pure air to breathe, so too does an engine. Air filters serve as the lungs of a vehicle, ensuring the air going into the engine is free of contaminants. But there's more; vehicles are also equipped with cabin air filters designed to purify the air we, the passengers, breathe while inside. Understanding the roles of these filters and the importance of their maintenance is essential for every car owner.

Imagine a scenario where you're jogging in a park, and suddenly, someone places a cloth over your mouth, making it hard to breathe. It's stifling, right? This situation mirrors what happens to an engine operating with a clogged air filter. A **dirty engine air filter** restricts the flow of air into the engine, thereby diminishing its efficiency. Reduced air intake means the engine must work harder, resulting in reduced fuel efficiency and power. Over time, this strain can cause wear and tear, leading to costly repairs or even engine failure.

Now, while the engine air filter shields the engine, the **cabin air filter** protects the vehicle's occupants. It ensures the air inside the car is free from pollutants like pollen, dust, and even exhaust fumes. A blocked cabin filter can cause the air inside to become stale and filled with contaminants, potentially triggering allergies and respiratory issues.

So, how does one recognize the signs of a dirty filter? A noticeable decrease in mileage, a strange engine sound, or a foul odor emanating from the air vents can be indicative of filter issues. Black smoke from the exhaust is another tell-tale sign, as this indicates unburned fuel, which, in turn, points to a lack of adequate air in the combustion chamber.

For those eager to understand the replacement process, here's a basic overview:

1. **Engine Air Filter Replacement:** Begin by locating the air filter box, usually found on the top of the engine. It's typically a black plastic box. After opening it, you'll find the air filter, which is usually round or rectangular and made of paper or synthetic material. Examine it; if it's full of debris or darkened, it's time for a change. Swap the old with the new, ensuring it sits snugly. Lastly, close the box securely.

2. **Cabin Air Filter Replacement:** The location varies across vehicles but is often behind the glove compartment or under the dashboard. Upon locating, remove the old filter, take note of the direction of airflow (usually indicated by arrows), and install the new filter accordingly. Make sure it fits well, and then reassemble any parts you've disassembled.

Both filters should typically be checked every 12,000 to 15,000 miles, though it's wise to consult the owner's manual for specifics. Replacing them isn't just a maintenance task but an investment in the longevity of the engine and the health of the car's occupants.

In conclusion, understanding and maintaining the air filters in your vehicle are not tasks to be overlooked. They're straightforward yet crucial components that ensure the optimal functioning of the engine and a healthy in-car environment. Treat them with care, and they'll ensure your vehicle runs smoothly, efficiently, and is a pleasant space to be in.

With a grasp on air filters, our next segment will equip you with further essential knowledge, ensuring your vehicle remains in prime condition. As we delve deeper into vehicle maintenance, each chapter aims to empower you with the skills and understanding to confidently care for your vehicle.

Checking and Replacing Fluids

Every car functions as a symphony of mechanical parts, electronics, and crucially, fluids. Just as our bodies rely on blood, water, and other vital fluids to function optimally, vehicles need their assortment of liquids to keep running smoothly. In this segment, we'll dive deep into understanding these essential fluids, their roles, and the importance of regular maintenance to ensure your vehicle's longevity and efficiency.

Imagine for a moment a water pump in a garden. If you don't provide it with water, it'll run dry, resulting in damage. Similarly, cars have pumps, gears, and systems that rely on specific fluids. Failing to maintain these fluids can spell disaster for your vehicle.

Let's begin with the lifeblood of any engine: **engine oil**. This lubricates the engine's internal parts, preventing friction and wear. Dirty or low oil can lead to increased engine wear, decreased performance, and eventually, engine failure. Regularly checking the oil level using the dipstick and ensuring its clarity is paramount. Dark, gritty oil is an indicator that it needs changing.

Next, we have the **coolant**, which ensures your engine doesn't overheat. An engine operates at high temperatures, and without a proper cooling system filled with the right amount of coolant, it could overheat, causing significant damage. The coolant reservoir is typically transparent, allowing for easy level checks. Remember, never open a radiator cap when the engine is hot.

Transmission fluid is another crucial fluid, especially for automatic vehicles. It ensures that the gear shifts are smooth and reduces wear on the transmission's internal parts. Like engine oil, it should be clear, not burnt or dirty. Most cars have a transmission dipstick similar to the oil one, making it easy to check.

The **brake fluid** plays an indispensable role in ensuring your vehicle can stop properly. It transfers the pressure from your brake pedal to the brake calipers, allowing the brake pads to clamp down on the rotors. Low or dirty brake fluid can compromise braking efficiency or even lead to brake failure. Most vehicles have a brake fluid reservoir that you can visually inspect.

Power steering fluid ensures that turning your car's steering wheel feels smooth and not like a workout session. Low or dirty fluid can make steering difficult and noisy. Many cars have a dedicated reservoir with level markings for this fluid.

Lastly, there's **windshield washer fluid**. While it might not seem as critical as the others, anyone who's tried to clean a dirty windshield while driving will attest to its importance. A dedicated reservoir, often blue, is present, and refilling it is a breeze.

Allowing any of these fluids to run low or get dirty poses risks. From decreased performance and efficiency to more severe consequences like engine failure or even accidents due to brake inefficiency. Regular checks, ideally monthly, are a small investment of time that can prevent potentially costly and dangerous issues down the road.

In wrapping up, understanding and maintaining your vehicle's fluids isn't just a task for mechanics. It's something every car owner can and should do. Familiarize yourself with your vehicle, refer to its manual, and take proactive steps to ensure it runs smoothly. With a little attention and care, your car will reward you with reliable service and performance.

As we continue our journey into car maintenance, our next chapter will delve into another aspect vital for ensuring your vehicle remains in top shape. With each section, our goal is to make you a more informed and confident car owner, ready to tackle challenges head-on.

Tire Maintenance

For a vehicle, tires are what shoes are to us – an indispensable connection to the ground, bearing the full weight, and responsible for enabling movement. In this expansive chapter, we're delving deep into tire maintenance, illuminating its crucial importance and the risks associated with neglecting it.

Picture this: walking miles in shoes with worn-out soles. The discomfort is one thing, but the potential for trips, falls, and other mishaps is an undeniable reality. Similarly, vehicles with tires in subpar condition are a risk to safety, fuel efficiency, and the general driving experience.

Tread Depth: At the very heart of tire safety is the tread depth. The tread, characterized by the patterned outer surface of the tire, is designed for optimum grip on various road conditions. As miles accumulate, this tread inevitably wears down. When tread depth decreases, the tire's grip on wet roads diminishes, increasing braking distances and the risk of aquaplaning. Many drivers are familiar with the penny test to measure tread depth: inserting a penny into the tread with Lincoln's head facing down. If the top of Lincoln's head remains visible, your tire is shouting for a replacement. But, a more accurate method is using a **tread depth gauge**, which provides a precise measurement and helps in making informed decisions.

Tire Pressure

Maintaining the correct tire pressure is paramount not only for the longevity of your tires but also for safety and fuel efficiency. Tire pressure is measured in pounds per square inch (PSI) in the US, or in bars or kilopascals in other parts of the world.

1. **Understanding the Right Pressure**: The first step in maintaining tire pressure is to understand the recommended PSI for your vehicle. This information can typically be found in the vehicle's owner manual. Another common place is the sticker inside the driver's side door or fuel hatch. Different vehicles have varying requirements, so always refer to these sources rather than the maximum pressure level indicated on the tire sidewall.

    - **Common PSI Range for Passenger Cars**: Most typical passenger cars recommend a tire pressure in the range of 32 to 35 PSI. However, larger vehicles like SUVs and trucks might have a different range. Always prioritize the manufacturer's recommendation over general guidelines.

2. **Checking the Pressure**: To check your tire pressure, you'll need a **tire pressure gauge**. There are different types of gauges: pencil, dial, and digital. The digital type is often preferred for its accuracy and ease of reading.

   - **Procedure**: Remove the cap from the tire's valve stem. Press the tire gauge onto the valve stem for a few seconds. If you hear a hissing sound, it means air is escaping. Adjust and press harder until the hissing stops, and a reading appears on the gauge. Note the reading.

3. **Adjusting the Pressure**: If the tire pressure is either too high or too low based on the manufacturer's recommendation:

   - **Inflating**: If the reading is below the recommended PSI, inflate the tire. Most gas stations are equipped with air pumps. Attach the air hose to the valve stem. As you add air, frequently check the pressure using the gauge to avoid over-inflation.

   - **Deflating**: If the tire is over-inflated, press the inside pin of the valve stem to release some air. Check the pressure intermittently to ensure you don't deflate too much.

4. **Factors Affecting Tire Pressure**: The outside temperature can affect tire pressure. For every 10°F change in temperature, tire pressure changes about 1 PSI. Tires tend to lose more pressure in cold conditions. This is why it's crucial to check tire pressure with changing seasons, especially transitioning from summer to winter.

5. **Frequency**: For optimal performance and safety, it's advised to check your tire pressure at least once a month and before long trips. This includes checking the spare tire as well.

6. **Benefits of Proper Tire Pressure**:

   - **Safety**: Correct tire pressure ensures that the vehicle's weight is evenly distributed across the tire's tread pattern. This uniformity improves the car's handling and responsiveness.

   - **Fuel Efficiency**: Under-inflated tires have more rolling resistance, requiring more energy (fuel) to move the vehicle.

   - **Tire Longevity**: Properly inflated tires wear more evenly, extending their lifespan and saving money over time.

In summary, keeping your tires at the right pressure is a relatively simple procedure, but its benefits are vast. It's an essential routine to ensure safety, save money, and reduce your carbon footprint. By understanding your vehicle's specific requirements and frequently checking and adjusting the pressure, you can enjoy a smoother, safer drive.

Rotation: The topic of tire rotation isn't just about ensuring even wear. Rotation patterns might vary based on whether your vehicle is front-wheel drive, rear-wheel drive, all-wheel drive, or if the tires are directional. Generally, for front-wheel-drive vehicles, the front tires should move straight to the rear, and the rear tires should move to the front but switch sides. This might sound complex, but it's a routine procedure at any garage. Depending on driving conditions and tire quality, the rotation should ideally be done every 6,000 to 8,000 miles.

Tire Replacement and Hazards

Replacing a tire can be a demanding task, especially for novices, but with the right tools and a step-by-step approach, it's manageable. Moreover, being aware of potential hazards can prevent accidents and ensure safety throughout the process.

Tools Needed for Tire Replacement:

1. **Jack:** To lift the vehicle off the ground.

2. **Lug Wrench:** For removing and securing the lug nuts.

3. **Spare Tire:** Ensure it's properly inflated.

4. **Wheel Chocks:** To keep the vehicle from rolling.

5. **Gloves:** To protect your hands.

6. **Torch or Flashlight:** In case you need to change a tire in the dark.

Instructions:

1. **Safety First:** Before you start, park the vehicle on a stable, flat surface away from traffic. Engage the parking brake and, if available, use wheel chocks to secure the opposite end of the vehicle you'll be jacking up.

2. **Remove Hubcap or Wheel Cover (if applicable):** If your car has hubcaps or wheel covers, remove them to access the lug nuts. Usually, the flat end of your lug wrench can help pop these off.

3. **Loosening the Lug Nuts:** With the tire still on the ground, use the lug wrench to loosen (but not fully remove) the lug nuts in a crisscross pattern. This initial loosening prevents the wheel from spinning when elevated.

4. **Positioning the Jack**: Refer to your vehicle's manual to identify the correct jack points. Once you've found the appropriate point, place the jack underneath and ensure it's stable.

5. **Raising the Vehicle**: Jack up the vehicle slowly. Ensure the jack remains straight and securely in the jacking point as the car rises.

6. **Remove Lug Nuts and Tire**: Once the vehicle is elevated, finish removing the lug nuts and then take off the flat tire. Remember, tires can be heavy, so be careful while handling them.

7. **Mount the Spare Tire**: Position the spare tire on the hub, aligning the rim with the lug bolts. Push the tire onto the car until it can't go any further.

8. **Hand-tighten the Lug Nuts**: Before lowering the vehicle, hand-tighten the lug nuts as much as possible in a crisscross pattern.

9. **Lower the Vehicle**: Slowly lower the vehicle using the jack. Once on the ground, remove the jack.

10. **Fully Tighten the Lug Nuts**: With the vehicle stable, use the lug wrench to fully tighten the lug nuts, again in a crisscross pattern. Ensure they are securely tightened to prevent the tire from coming off while driving.

11. **Store All Equipment**: Place the flat tire, jack, lug wrench, and any other tools back in the vehicle.

12. **Check Tire Pressure**: Before driving off, check the pressure in the spare tire to ensure it's safe to drive on. Remember, some spare tires are meant for temporary use and may have speed and distance limitations.

Hazards and Safety Precautions:

1. **Incorrect Jack Placement**: Using the wrong jack point can damage your vehicle or cause the car to fall. Always refer to the owner's manual.

2. **Loose Lug Nuts**: Failing to properly tighten lug nuts can result in a tire coming off while driving.

3. **Using a Damaged or Flat Spare**: Always ensure your spare is in good condition and properly inflated.

4. **Safety on the Roadside**: If you need to change a tire on the road, always use hazard lights, and if available, reflective triangles or flares to alert other drivers.

5. **Handling of Jack**: Use caution when raising and lowering the jack to avoid sudden movements that can destabilize the car.

In conclusion, changing a tire is a valuable skill that every driver should have. Though it might seem challenging initially, with practice and attention to safety, it becomes a straightforward task.

Regularly inspecting your tires for wear and keeping essential tools in good condition can make the process smoother when the need arises.

Consequences of negligence span from the obvious, such as reduced fuel efficiency and uneven tire wear, to the severe, like tire blowouts which can lead to major accidents. Handling abilities decline with poor tire conditions, and braking distances increase, all potentially putting lives in jeopardy.

In conclusion, tires are pivotal to your vehicle's performance and safety. Their regular care and maintenance can't be emphasized enough. The ideal practice is a holistic approach, incorporating regular checks, timely rotations, and understanding when replacements are due.

As we gear up to delve deeper into the intricacies of vehicle maintenance, remember that a well-maintained vehicle isn't just about performance – it's about safety, longevity, and overall driving pleasure. Up next, we'll explore more components and systems, ensuring you're equipped with comprehensive knowledge for optimal vehicle care.

Checking Tire Pressure

Tire pressure is one of those aspects of vehicle maintenance that can often go overlooked, yet it holds paramount importance. It's akin to our own blood pressure - just as you wouldn't want it too high or too low, the same goes for your tires. Understanding, checking, and maintaining the right tire pressure not only ensures the longevity of your tires but also guarantees optimal vehicle performance and safety.

So, why does **tire pressure** matter so much? Firstly, the pressure inside your tires affects the amount of contact the rubber has with the road. When the tire is under-inflated, more rubber touches the ground, leading to increased friction. This can cause the tire to wear out faster, and it can even overheat, leading to potential blowouts. On the other hand, an over-inflated tire has less rubber contact, decreasing its grip on the road and making it more prone to damage from potholes or debris.

Moreover, maintaining the correct tire pressure can lead to better gas mileage. An under-inflated tire can decrease fuel efficiency, meaning more frequent stops at the gas station and an unwanted strain on your wallet. On the safety front, improperly inflated tires can alter your car's handling and braking, putting you and your passengers at risk.

Now, to the heart of the matter: **how do you check and adjust tire pressure?**

Tools Needed:

1. **Tire Pressure Gauge**: A small device that can either be digital or analog. It measures the air pressure inside the tires.

2. **Air Compressor**: Found at most gas stations or can be a personal device for inflating tires.

Instructions:

1. **Start Cold**: It's best to check tire pressure when the tires are cold, meaning they've been stationary for at least three hours. This gives the most accurate reading as tires heat up when driven, which can inflate the pressure reading.

2. **Locate the Recommended Pressure**: Before you start, identify the recommended tire pressure for your vehicle. This information is typically found inside the driver's door frame, in the owner's manual, or sometimes on the tire itself. It's expressed in **PSI (Pounds per Square Inch)**.

3. **Remove the Tire Valve Cap**: On each tire, there's a small cap on the valve stem. Unscrew and set it aside, but remember where you place it as it's crucial for protecting the valve from debris and moisture.

4. **Use the Gauge**: Push the tire pressure gauge onto the valve stem. If you're using an analog gauge, a small bar will pop out from the bottom, displaying the tire's pressure. For a digital gauge, simply read the number on the display.

5. **Adjust if Necessary**: If the reading is above or below the recommended PSI, adjust accordingly. If it's too high, press the gauge down slightly on the valve stem to release some air. If it's too low, add air using an air compressor until you reach the recommended PSI.

6. **Replace the Valve Cap**: Once you're done, screw the cap back onto the valve stem.

7. **Repeat**: Carry out this process for all four tires, and don't forget the spare if you have one.

It's advisable to check your tire pressure at least once a month and before long trips. Tires can naturally lose 1-2 PSI per month, and this rate can increase with temperature fluctuations.

In wrapping up this chapter, the importance of maintaining the proper tire pressure cannot be overemphasized. Not only does it assure you of a smoother drive, but it also ensures you're driving efficiently and safely.

As we transition into Chapter 5, we'll delve deeper into **Intermediate Maintenance Procedures**. This will cover more intricate aspects of car care, from understanding the braking system to demystifying the world of car fuses. Stay tuned to elevate your auto maintenance knowledge even further.

Chapter 5: Intermediate Maintenance Procedures

Brake Maintenance

From the moment you turn your car's ignition on to the time you come to a stop at your destination, every part of your vehicle serves a purpose. But, arguably, none is as vital to your safety as your car's **brake system**. This intricate combination of components ensures that you can stop your vehicle efficiently and safely. In this chapter, we'll delve into the essentials of brake maintenance, focusing primarily on the replacement of brake pads and rotors.

Imagine for a moment a scenario where you're cruising down the highway and a sudden obstacle appears. Your heart races, and instinctively, you step on the brake pedal. Now, consider what might happen if your brakes were worn out or malfunctioning. The results could be catastrophic. Thus, understanding the condition and performance of your brake system is not just a matter of car upkeep, but a matter of life and safety.

Let's begin by understanding the core components:

1. **Brake Pads**: These are the friction material that gets pressed against the rotors to create the resistance needed to stop your vehicle. Over time, with continuous application, they wear down and need to be replaced.

2. **Rotors**: Also known as brake discs, these are the parts that the brake pads press against. When the brake pedal is depressed, the pads squeeze the rotors, which in turn slows and eventually stops the wheel.

Brake Pads and Rotors Replacement Guide:

Tools Needed:

- **Jack and jack stands**: To lift the car safely.

- **Wrench set**: To remove the caliper.

- **C-clamp or brake caliper tool**: To push the piston back in.

- **New brake pads and rotors**: Ensure they're the right fit for your vehicle.

Instructions:

1. **Safety First**: Before you begin, ensure the car is on a flat surface. Put on safety gloves and goggles.

2. **Lift the Car**: Use the jack to lift the vehicle, then securely position the jack stands underneath.

3. **Remove the Wheel**: Using the appropriate wrench, remove the lug nuts and take off the wheel, exposing the brake components.

4. **Locate the Caliper**: This component covers the brake pads and is bolted to the rotor.

5. **Remove the Caliper**: Using a wrench, carefully unbolt the caliper. Once it's free, don't let it hang by the brake line; this can damage it. Instead, place it on a nearby stand or hang it with a piece of wire.

6. **Take Out the Old Brake Pads**: Now, you should be able to slide the old brake pads out. Note how they're positioned for when you replace them with the new ones.

7. **Replace the Rotor**: If you're changing the rotors, now's the time. Remove the old rotor and replace it with the new one. If it's stuck due to rust or debris, a gentle tap with a rubber mallet can help.

8. **Install the New Brake Pads**: Slide the new pads into the same position as the old ones.

9. **Reposition the Caliper**: Before you do, use the C-clamp or brake caliper tool to push the piston back in. This makes room for the new, thicker pads. Once done, bolt the caliper back into place.

10. **Reattach the Wheel**: Place the wheel back, securing it with the lug nuts.

11. **Lower the Car**: Carefully remove the jack stands and lower your car.

12. **Test**: Before you drive off, press the brake pedal a few times. It should feel firm. This ensures the brake fluid has reached the calipers and that the brake pads are properly positioned.

Hazards of Neglecting Brake Maintenance:

When you neglect your brake system, not only do you compromise safety, but you also risk expensive repairs. Worn-out brake pads can cause damage to the rotors, leading to vibrations when braking. Moreover, if the brake fluid gets contaminated, it can lead to brake failure, as the fluid won't be able to exert the necessary pressure.

In summary, your vehicle's brake system is its most crucial safety feature. Regular inspections and timely replacements of worn-out parts can save not only money but also lives. As you transition from basic to more intricate maintenance procedures, understanding and caring for your brakes stands as a foundational skill.

Coming up in the next chapter, we'll venture into other **Intermediate Maintenance Procedures**. We'll demystify components that often go overlooked but play a significant role in your car's overall health and efficiency. Stay tuned, and let's continue this journey of automotive discovery together.

Bleeding Brake Lines

Ensuring that your car's brakes function at their best is not just about maintaining brake pads and rotors; it also involves the meticulous upkeep of your vehicle's brake lines. Within these lines, hydraulic fluid works as a medium to transmit the force from your foot on the brake pedal to the brakes themselves. Sometimes, however, air bubbles can get trapped in these lines, leading to spongy brakes and reduced performance. The solution to this problem is a procedure known as **bleeding brake lines**.

At the core, bleeding brake lines means removing any trapped air from the hydraulic system. But why is this necessary? Think of these air bubbles as unwanted visitors in a system that thrives on consistency and precision. When you depress the brake pedal, hydraulic fluid exerts pressure to apply the brakes. Air, being compressible unlike hydraulic fluid, can compromise this pressure, making your brakes feel spongy and reducing their responsiveness. This can be dangerous, especially in situations requiring sudden braking.

Now, let's dive into the step-by-step guide to bleed your brake lines:

Tools and Supplies Needed:

- **Brake fluid**: Check your vehicle's manual for the specific type recommended.

- **Clear plastic tubing**: To direct old brake fluid into a container.

- **Wrench**: To open the bleeder valves.

- **Brake bleeder kit**: While not mandatory, this can simplify the process.

- **Empty container**: For collecting old brake fluid.

- **Helper**: Someone to press the brake pedal.

Instructions:

1. **Safety Preparations**: Before starting, ensure that the vehicle is on level ground and the ignition is off. Wear gloves and safety glasses to protect yourself from any brake fluid splashes.

2. **Locate the Bleeder Valves**: Typically found behind each wheel, these small valves allow you to release trapped air and old brake fluid. Starting with the wheel farthest from the master cylinder (usually the rear passenger wheel), locate its bleeder valve.

3. **Prepare to Collect Fluid**: Connect the clear plastic tubing to the bleeder valve and place the other end into an empty container. This will allow you to see air bubbles as they come out and keep brake fluid from spilling.

4. **Press the Brake Pedal**: Have your helper press down on the brake pedal and hold it there.

5. **Open the Bleeder Valve**: While the pedal is being pressed, open the valve with a wrench. Fluid, and hopefully air bubbles, will flow out through the tubing.

6. **Close the Valve and Release the Pedal**: Once the fluid flows steadily without bubbles, close the valve. Only after the valve is closed should your helper release the brake pedal. This avoids sucking back in any air.

7. **Repeat for Each Wheel**: Use the same method for each wheel, moving closer to the master cylinder with each bleed.

8. **Check the Brake Fluid Reservoir**: During this process, the brake fluid level can drop. Periodically check the reservoir and top it up with fresh brake fluid to prevent air from getting sucked into the master cylinder.

9. **Test the Brakes**: Once you've bled all the lines, ask your helper to press the brake pedal several times. It should feel firm and not spongy. If it still feels soft, you might need to repeat the bleeding process.

10. **Dispose of Old Brake Fluid**: Remember, brake fluid is hazardous and should be disposed of properly. Never pour it down the drain or into the ground.

In conclusion, bleeding brake lines might seem daunting at first, but with the right tools and a bit of patience, it's an attainable skill for most car owners. This procedure not only ensures that your brakes are responsive and efficient but also can add to the longevity of your brake system. By regularly checking and maintaining all components, including the brake lines, you ensure the safety of your vehicle's occupants and those around you.

Up next in our journey into car maintenance, we'll be delving into further advanced topics. Chapter 6 introduces you to **Intermediate Maintenance Procedures** that provide an in-depth look at some components that often go unnoticed. Keeping the momentum going, let's turn the page to continue refining your automotive knowledge.

Replacing Spark Plugs and Wires

In the world of automotive mechanics, **spark plugs** and their accompanying wires might appear as small components, but they play a pivotal role in the smooth functioning of an internal combustion engine. The spark plug, as its name suggests, produces a spark to ignite the fuel-air mixture in the engine's combustion chamber, thus powering your vehicle. As with many car components, these too have a lifespan, after which replacement becomes necessary for optimal performance.

But why does such a seemingly simple component need attention? Over time, spark plugs can wear out or become fouled due to deposits. When this happens, your engine might not run efficiently. The wires, on the other hand, transport the electrical charge to the spark plug. If they're damaged or worn out, this can result in a weak spark or no spark at all.

Now, what are the symptoms that might indicate it's time for a replacement? A few common signs include:

- Difficulty starting your car.

- Noticeable decrease in fuel efficiency.

- Engine misfires or rough idling.

- Reduced acceleration or a noticeable drop in engine performance.

- Unusual or consistent noises from the engine.

If you've observed any of the above symptoms, it might be time to inspect and possibly replace your spark plugs and wires. So, let's walk through the process:

Tools and Supplies Needed:

- **Spark plug socket and wrench**: Specifically designed for removing and installing spark plugs.

- **Spark plug gap gauge**: To check and adjust the gap between the electrode and ground.

- **Dielectric grease**: Aids in protecting the plug boot from sticking to the spark plug.

- **Anti-seize compound**: Helps ensure easy removal of the spark plug in the future.

- **New spark plugs and wires**: Always refer to your vehicle's manual for the right type.

Instructions:

1. **Safety First**: Before starting, ensure the engine is cool. A hot engine can make removing spark plugs difficult and even risky. Disconnect the battery's negative terminal for added safety.

2. **Identify and Remove Old Spark Plugs**: Locate the spark plugs. They are typically found on the engine's top or side, with wires attached. Carefully pull the wire boot off the spark plug (do not pull by the wire) and use your spark plug socket to unscrew and remove the old spark plug.

3. **Inspect the Old Spark Plug**: This step, while not mandatory for replacement, can provide insights into engine health. Deposits, erosion, or an oily spark plug can be indicative of larger issues.

4. **Prepare the New Spark Plug**: Using the spark plug gap gauge, adjust the new spark plug gap as specified in your vehicle's manual. Apply a small amount of anti-seize compound to the threads.

5. **Install the New Spark Plug**: Carefully screw in the spark plug by hand until snug. Then, using the wrench, tighten it but avoid over-tightening, which can damage the threads.

6. **Replace the Wire (if necessary)**: If replacing the spark plug wire, it's best to do them one at a time to keep track. Apply dielectric grease to the inside of the new boot, then attach the wire to the spark plug and the distributor or ignition coil.

7. **Repeat for All Cylinders**: It's crucial to replace all spark plugs, even if only one shows signs of wear, to ensure even performance.

8. **Reconnect Battery and Test**: Once you've replaced all spark plugs and wires, reconnect the battery and start the car. Listen to the engine; it should run smoothly.

Maintaining or replacing spark plugs and wires might appear daunting initially, but with the right tools and some patience, it's an entirely achievable task. Doing so not only ensures optimal performance but can also contribute to extended engine life and improved fuel economy. As we venture further into the world of car maintenance, understanding these foundational elements prepares you for more advanced topics.

In the next chapter, we'll delve into even deeper terrains of vehicle maintenance, addressing more intricate components that play a critical role in your car's performance. Join us in Chapter 6 as we unfold the mysteries behind **Advanced Maintenance Procedures**. The journey continues, and every step takes us closer to mastering automotive care.

Cooling System Maintenance

For those familiar with the roaring sensation of an engine starting up or the smooth purr of a car cruising down a highway, it's clear that vehicles exert a tremendous amount of energy. But with all this energy comes heat, and if not managed correctly, this heat can spell disaster for an engine. That's where the **cooling system** steps in, serving as the unsung hero, preserving the engine's health and ensuring your vehicle runs optimally.

The cooling system's primary function is to regulate the temperature of the engine and prevent overheating. It achieves this by circulating coolant through the engine, absorbing the excess heat, and then dissipating it via the radiator. Neglecting this system can lead to overheating, resulting in engine damage, reduced efficiency, or, in worst-case scenarios, total engine failure. So, how can one maintain this vital system effectively?

1. Flushing and Filling the Radiator: The **radiator** is the cooling system's heart. Over time, the coolant circulating within can become contaminated with rust and scale deposits, which can impede its flow and reduce its heat-absorbing capacity.

- **Tools and Materials Needed**: Distilled water, coolant (usually a 50/50 mix of water and antifreeze), a drain pan, a funnel, radiator flush solution, wrench, and protective gloves.

- **Procedure**:

    - Begin with a cool engine. Ensure the vehicle has been stationary for hours, giving it ample time to cool down.

    - Place a drain pan beneath the radiator. Locate the drain valve or plug (usually at the radiator's bottom) and open it. Allow the old coolant to drain fully.

- Close the drain and fill the radiator with a radiator flush solution and distilled water. Start the engine, turn the heater on high, and let it run for as long as the flush product recommends (typically 10 minutes).

- Once done, turn off the engine, let it cool, and drain the flush solution.

- Refill the radiator with a 50/50 mix of coolant and distilled water. Make sure to fill it up to the recommended level.

- Start the engine again, let it run until it reaches its operating temperature, and check for any leaks.

2. Regularly Checking the Coolant Level: The coolant reservoir, a translucent container near the radiator, lets you see the coolant level without opening the radiator. It's wise to inspect this regularly. If the level drops frequently, it might indicate a leak in the system.

3. Inspecting Hoses and Belts: Hoses transport the coolant, while belts drive the water pump. Regularly inspect these for cracks, leaks, or signs of wear, ensuring that the coolant circulates effectively.

4. Thermostat Check: The **thermostat** controls the flow of the coolant, ensuring the engine warms up quickly and then maintains an optimal operating temperature. A malfunctioning thermostat can result in overheating or, conversely, an engine that doesn't warm up at all. If you notice such symptoms, consider checking or replacing the thermostat.

The consequences of neglecting the cooling system can be severe. Imagine driving on a hot summer day, and suddenly, steam billows from beneath the hood, indicating an overheated engine. Regular maintenance prevents such incidents, protecting your engine and ensuring a smoother driving experience.

In the journey of understanding our vehicle better, we've touched upon various essential components. As we transition to the next chapter, we'll explore further into the intricate world of automotive maintenance. Join us in Chapter 6 as we dive deeper into **Fuel System Care and Maintenance**. With each step, we equip ourselves with the knowledge to keep our beloved vehicles running at their best.

Battery Maintenance and Replacement

In the intricate orchestra of a car's components, the **battery** holds a pivotal role. It's the silent powerhouse that breathes life into the vehicle, setting every other part into motion. Just as a heart pumps blood to kickstart various bodily functions, the car battery dispatches necessary electrical energy, ensuring everything from ignition to lighting operates seamlessly. Understanding this component's workings, how to maintain it, and when to replace it is vital for every car owner.

The car battery, predominantly a lead-acid storage unit, is accountable for supplying short bursts of energy to the starter motor, igniting the engine, and providing power to other electrical accessories when the engine isn't running. Without it, well, your car wouldn't even start.

One might wonder, "How do I ensure my battery is always in top shape?" Regular maintenance is the answer. While car batteries are designed to be robust and durable, they aren't infallible and demand periodic attention.

1. Regular Inspection and Cleaning: Over time, corrosion can build up on battery terminals, impairing the connection and leading to a decline in performance. By visually inspecting the battery, one can often identify if there's any buildup or if the battery shows signs of swelling. Cleaning the terminals using a mixture of baking soda and water, followed by a thorough rinse with cold water, can help combat this corrosion. Always remember to wear protective gloves and eyewear during this process.

2. Testing the Battery: A multimeter, a handy tool available at most automotive stores, can gauge your battery's health. A fully charged battery typically shows a reading of about 12.6 volts or higher. If the reading is below 12.2 volts, it indicates that the battery might be undercharged. On the contrary, if it reads above 12.9 volts when the car is off, it means the battery is overcharged, which can be equally damaging.

3. Recognizing Symptoms of a Failing Battery: Apart from using tools, staying alert to symptoms can give you a heads-up if the battery is nearing its end. Slow engine crank, dimming headlights, or the illumination of the battery warning light on the dashboard are clear indications. Additionally, a rotten egg smell might point towards a leaking battery, which needs immediate attention.

4. Replacing the Battery: If tests and symptoms indicate that the battery's health is dwindling, replacement might be on the cards. For this:

- First, identify a suitable replacement battery by checking your vehicle's manual for specifications.

- Ensure your vehicle is off. Wearing protective gloves, start by disconnecting the negative cable followed by the positive.

- Remove the battery holder or clamp and gently lift the battery out.

- Place the new battery in, ensuring it sits snugly. Reconnect the positive cable followed by the negative. It's crucial to avoid reversing this order.

Neglecting battery maintenance can land one in frustrating situations, like being stranded in a desolate parking lot with a car that refuses to start. It not only ensures smooth vehicle operation but also saves money and time in the long run.

As we wrap up this enlightening chapter on battery care, our journey into the realm of automotive knowledge deepens. As you transition to Chapter 6, titled **Advanced Repair Skills**, brace yourself for a deep dive into the more intricate and technical facets of car maintenance. Fear not, for every term will be broken down, ensuring you grasp concepts with ease, building upon the foundation we've laid thus far.

Chapter 6: Advanced Repair Skills

Changing the Timing Belt/Chain

Embarking on the journey of understanding vehicle components brings us to a critical, often overlooked element: the **timing belt/chain**. Serving as the conductor of the engine's orchestra, this component ensures the synchronization of the engine's camshaft and crankshaft. If the timing belt or chain fails, it could spell catastrophe for the engine, rendering your vehicle useless.

At a glance, the timing belt might seem like a mere strip, but its importance is paramount. It controls the engine's valves, ensuring they open and close at precise intervals. This synchronized dance allows the engine to breathe, making it vital for the combustion process. Now, let's elucidate why maintaining and, when necessary, replacing this component is so crucial.

Engines are classified into two types based on the aftermath of a timing belt failure: interference and non-interference engines. In interference engines, a timing belt failure could lead to valves being struck by pistons, causing significant engine damage. On the other hand, non-interference engines might escape with minimal harm, though the car will still come to a standstill. Understanding which type your car possesses can help you grasp the potential risks and damages of neglecting the timing belt or chain.

Now, let's dive into the specifics of replacing this component.

1. Recognize the Symptoms: The primary step is to detect when a replacement is imminent. A ticking noise from the engine, the engine not turning over, oil leakage from the front of the motor, or a misfiring engine could all point towards a worn-out timing belt or chain.

2. Gathering The Necessary Tools:

Before embarking on the task, having the right tools will ensure efficiency and safety. These are some of the fundamental tools and equipment you will need:

- **Repair Manual**: Specific to your vehicle's make and model. This will provide unique instructions and diagrams for your vehicle's engine.

- **Socket Set and Wrenches**: Various sizes are required to deal with the different nuts and bolts you'll encounter. Ratcheting wrenches can be particularly useful in the tight spaces you might have to work in.

- **Screwdrivers**: Both flathead and Phillips may be necessary for removing covers or securing parts.

- **Timing Light**: Essential for checking that your engine's timing is correctly set after replacing the belt or chain.

- **Torque Wrench**: This ensures that bolts, especially those on the engine, are tightened to the manufacturer's specifications.

- **White Marker or Chalk**: To mark the position of the camshaft and crankshaft pulleys if there are no existing markings.

- **Jack and Jack Stands**: Necessary if you need to elevate the car to access the underside of the engine.

- **Gloves and Safety Goggles**: To protect against accidental splashes of coolant or oil and to ensure a firm grip on tools.

3. The Replacement:

The task is meticulous but with patience, it's achievable. Here's an in-depth breakdown:

- **Safety Precautions**: Begin on a flat surface. With gloves and safety goggles on, disconnect the negative terminal of the car's battery to avoid electrical mishaps.

- **Gaining Access**:
    1. Start by removing the serpentine belt that powers multiple devices in the engine.
    2. Engine accessories, such as the alternator, power steering pump, and air conditioning compressor, may need to be detached. Once they're out of your way, remove the timing cover.

- **Timing Markings**:
    1. Note the positions of the camshaft and crankshaft pulleys. Use your white marker or chalk if there aren't pre-existing marks.
    2. These markings are crucial for ensuring accurate engine timing when installing the new belt or chain.

- **Dealing with the Tensioner and Old Belt/Chain**:

  1. Use your wrench to adjust the tensioner to release the pressure on the belt or chain. This device maintains the belt or chain's tension, ensuring it functions correctly.

  2. Once it's loosened, you can remove the old belt or chain.

- **Pulley and Tensioner Check**: Inspect the pulleys and tensioners. Any signs of wear, misalignment, or damage means they need replacing or realigning.

- **Installation of the New Belt/Chain**:

  1. Ensure the timing marks are aligned.

  2. Start from the crankshaft, and move to the camshaft, keeping the belt or chain taut.

  3. Slowly release the tensioner so it applies pressure, ensuring the correct tension on the belt or chain.

- **Verifying Timing Alignment**: Manually rotate the crankshaft pulley twice using a wrench, then verify that the timing marks on the pulleys align. Misalignment means readjustment is necessary.

- **Reassembly**: Reverse the disassembly steps. Attach the timing cover back, followed by engine components, and lastly the serpentine belt.

- **Battery and Testing**: Reconnect the battery. Start the engine and listen. A smooth running engine without unusual noises indicates a successful replacement.

Though these guidelines are comprehensive, they're general. Always consult the manufacturer's manual or a trusted vehicle-specific guide for precision during such tasks.

After replacement, it's prudent to run the engine for a few minutes, ensuring the belt operates without hitches and the engine runs smoothly.

In essence, the timing belt or chain is like the conductor of an orchestra, ensuring every component of the engine plays its part in harmony. Neglecting its maintenance can lead to off-tune performances, if not complete engine failure.

As we close this chapter, we prepare to delve even deeper into the realm of vehicle components and maintenance in the chapters to come. Your journey of understanding, maintaining, and possibly repairing your vehicle is well underway, and the road ahead promises to be enlightening.

Clutch Replacement in Manual Transmissions

Within manual vehicles, the **clutch** serves as an essential intermediary between the engine and the transmission system, facilitating gear shifts and ensuring a seamless transfer of power. Its paramount importance to the vehicle's performance means that wear or damage to the clutch can have significant ramifications. Here, we provide an in-depth guide on clutch replacement, designed to navigate both seasoned mechanics and new enthusiasts through the process.

Symptoms of a Failing Clutch:

- **Spongy or Soft Clutch Pedal**: This sensation underfoot suggests that the clutch isn't releasing as it should, possibly due to air in the hydraulic line.

- **Difficulty in Shifting Gears**: If the clutch doesn't release properly, it can be challenging to switch between gears. This might manifest as a grinding noise or resistance.

- **Grinding or Screeching Noises**: Unfamiliar noises when the clutch pedal is depressed can signal issues with the clutch release bearing or the pilot bearing.

- **Vehicle Moving Despite Clutch Engagement**: This phenomenon, termed clutch drag, indicates that the clutch isn't disengaging when the pedal is pressed, causing the car to move even when the pedal is to the floor.

- **Burning Smell**: An unpleasant smell, likened to burning paper, can be a tell-tale sign of an overheating clutch, usually due to excessive slippage.

Step-by-Step Guide:

1. Preparation:

a. **Work Environment**: Identify a spacious and adequately illuminated workspace. This ensures safety and adequate maneuverability.

b. **Safety First**: Always wear safety goggles and durable gloves to protect against dirt, grease, and any unforeseen accidents.

2. Tool Gathering:

a. **Jack and Jack Stands**: Essential for elevating the vehicle, allowing for easy access to the undercarriage.

b. **Comprehensive Socket Set & Wrenches**: A variety of sizes ensures you're equipped to remove any bolt or nut.

c. **Screwdrivers**: Multiple sizes will come handy for disconnecting linkages and removing covers.

d. **Clutch Alignment Tool**: Vital for aligning the new clutch disc with the flywheel during installation.

e. **Torque Wrench**: To tighten bolts to the manufacturer's specifications, ensuring a safe reassembly.

f. **Brake Cleaner**: Useful for cleaning any residues or contaminants.

g. **Catch Pan**: To collect any fluids that may spill during the process.

h. **Organization Containers**: Trays or containers help to categorize and remember the placement of bolts and other components.

3. Disconnecting the Battery:

Safety Precaution: Always start by detaching the negative terminal. This step helps prevent unintentional electrical shorts.

4. Elevating the Car:

a. **Safe Lifting**: Use the jack to raise the front of the car. This allows for unhindered access to the transmission.

b. **Stability**: Position the jack stands under the vehicle to ensure it remains raised securely.

5. Accessing the Transmission:

a. **Gear Shift Linkage**: It's a connecting mechanism that transfers the driver's gear selection to the transmission. Detach it gently.

b. **Driveshaft Removal**: Disconnect this component, which transfers engine power to the vehicle's wheels.

c. **Sensors and Wires**: Detach all electronic connections related to the transmission. Label or photograph their positions for easier reassembly.

d. **Bolt Organization**: As you remove bolts, place them in labeled containers to ease the reassembly process.

6. Removing the Transmission:

a. **Unbolting**: With care, separate the transmission from the engine by removing all connecting bolts.

b. **Transmission Handling**: When setting aside, be aware that transmission fluid might drip. Use a pan to catch it.

7. Accessing and Removing the Clutch Assembly:

a. **Familiarization**: Identify the clutch disc, pressure plate, and flywheel, understanding their orientations.

b. **Pressure Plate**: Begin the removal process here. Beneath it, the clutch disc should slide out effortlessly.

c. **Orientation**: Remember or photograph the clutch disc's direction for correct placement later.

d. **Flywheel Inspection**: Check for damages like deep grooves or burn spots. Consider either resurfacing or replacement if wear is detected.

8. Installing the New Clutch:

a. **Placement**: Fit the new clutch disc onto the flywheel, making sure to match the previous orientation.

b. **Alignment**: With the clutch alignment tool, ensure the new disc aligns perfectly with the center of the flywheel before bolting the pressure plate into position.

9. Reassembly:

a. **Transmission**: Carefully reintroduce the transmission, ensuring it sits in alignment with the new clutch disc.

b. **Linkages and Driveshaft**: Reconnect the previously detached components, ensuring they fit snugly.

c. **Electrical Connections**: Reattach all sensors and wires to their original locations.

d. **Tightening**: Use the torque wrench to ensure all components are tightened to the manufacturer's specifications.

10. Testing the New Clutch

a. **Reconnect and Start**: With the car safely on the ground, reconnect the battery, turn the vehicle on, and test the clutch's responsiveness.

b. **Evaluation**: A smooth transition between gears and a firm clutch pedal indicates a successful replacement.

In summation, a clutch replacement might seem daunting but, with meticulous planning and an organized approach, even those unfamiliar with auto mechanics can achieve a successful replacement. Following this guide ensures not just the enhancement of the vehicle's performance but also its prolonged lifespan.

Suspension Work

The car's suspension system, though seemingly intricate with its metal rods and rubber joints, fundamentally ensures you a smooth journey by maintaining consistent tire contact with the road. This intricate dance involves key components like **struts** and **shocks**. In this chapter, we'll dive deeper into the roles of these pivotal components and offer a detailed, step-by-step guide on their replacement.

Imagine cruising without a proper suspension. Each road irregularity, no matter how minor, would amplify, making driving not only uncomfortable but also potentially damaging to other car components. With a compromised suspension system, tires might lose consistent contact with the road, leading to potential safety hazards, especially when navigating sharp turns or during abrupt stops.

If your vehicle seems more sensitive to bumps, leans excessively during turns, or oscillates after a bump rather than settling down, it's probably time for a suspension check. Remember, this isn't merely about enhancing driving comfort—it's fundamentally about safety. With that in mind, let's embark on the replacement procedure:

Suspension Replacement Guide:

1. **Preparation**

   - Ensure the vehicle is on a flat and stable surface.

   - Use a jack to lift the vehicle. For added safety, place the car on jack stands, providing a dual safeguard against any accidental drops.

2. **Tools You'll Need**

   - Regular wrench set

   - Spring compressors: These are essential when working with struts, allowing for the safe disassembly by compressing the potent springs they contain. A word of caution: springs under tension can be dangerous. Always abide by safety guidelines when employing spring compressors.

3. **Identifying Worn Out Struts and Shocks**

Before diving into the replacement procedure, it's essential to know when they need replacing. Telltale signs include:

   - A notably rougher or bouncy ride.

- The vehicle "nose dives" when you apply the brakes.

- Uneven tire wear, indicating the tires aren't maintaining consistent contact with the road.

- Visible damage or leakages from the struts or shocks.

Ignoring these signs can compromise your vehicle's handling and increase stopping distances, particularly in emergency situations.

4. **Replacement Process**

The heart of the task lies in the replacement process. Let's delve into a more granular exploration of the steps to ensure precision and safety:

Wheel Removal:

- Begin by removing the lug nuts from the wheel using a lug wrench. Ensure the wrench fits securely to avoid stripping the nuts.

- Once the lug nuts are loosened, completely remove them and then take off the wheel, setting it aside in a location where it won't obstruct your movement or roll away.

Identification of Struts/Shocks:

- With the wheel off, you'll get a clear view of the suspension system. Struts are typically larger and combine the spring and shock into one unit, while shocks are smaller, cylindrical components.

- Make a visual inspection to spot any noticeable wear, rust, or damage on the components or surrounding areas.

Safe Removal of Old Components:

- **Struts**: Before touching the strut, attach your spring compressors. This step is crucial because the tension in the springs can be dangerous. Attach the compressors opposite each other and tighten evenly. This ensures the spring compresses uniformly and reduces the risk of it releasing energy unpredictably.

- With the spring safely compressed, you can start by loosening the bolts securing the strut to the suspension system. These might be rusted or tightly fixed, so using a penetrating oil can assist in easier removal. Once loosened, carefully extract the strut.

- **Shocks**: The process is more straightforward for shocks. Identify the bolts or fasteners holding it in place. Once identified, use your wrench to gradually loosen and then fully remove them. Slide the old shock out from its mountings.

Installation of the New Component:

- **Struts**: Begin by cautiously decompressing the spring from the old strut using the spring compressors. Then, place it onto the new strut, ensuring it sits as it was on the original. Gradually release the spring compressors, letting the spring expand and settle into its new position. Once safely in place, the new strut can be bolted back to the suspension system. It's imperative to use a torque wrench and tighten to the manufacturer's specifications to ensure safety and correct function.

- **Shocks**: Slide the new shock into the mountings where the old one was. Secure it with the bolts or fasteners, ensuring they're tightened to the manufacturer's recommended torque settings.

Inspection:

- Before replacing the wheel, take a moment to inspect your work. Ensure all fastenings are secure, and there's no misalignment. Any inconsistencies can lead to reduced performance or potential safety hazards.

This thorough and meticulous process ensures the heart of your vehicle's suspension system is refreshed and robust, promising both comfort and safety in your driving experience.

5. **Finishing Up**

- Once you've securely attached the new struts or shocks, replace the wheel.

- Lower the vehicle from the jack stands carefully, ensuring everything is stable.

- It's advisable to test drive the vehicle in a safe area to ensure everything feels right and the issue is resolved.

By dedicating time to understand and uphold your car's suspension system, you're not just guaranteeing smoother drives but also significantly bolstering the safety and lifespan of your car. As we tread further into this guide, be prepared to delve into even more comprehensive automotive subjects, all tailored to equip you with a thorough grasp of car mechanics.

And as you close this chapter, proficiently equipped with the knowledge to replace struts and shocks, it paves the path to our next topic. In **Chapter 7**, we shall delve into the nuances of **Wheel Alignment and Tire Health**, further enhancing the safety and longevity of your vehicle. A well-aligned wheel not only ensures a straight drive but also plays a pivotal role in tire preservation. But more on that in the next chapter. Stay tuned!

Replacing Struts and Shocks

As you delve deeper into vehicle maintenance, one of the pivotal components to address is the vehicle's suspension system, particularly the **struts** and **shocks**. Both of these components play an instrumental role in ensuring a smooth ride, providing stability, and contributing to your vehicle's overall safety.

Struts and shocks might sound like fancy car jargon, but in simpler terms, think of them as the cushions that absorb the bumps and dips you encounter on the road. They not only help you ride comfortably but also ensure your tires remain in constant contact with the road, enhancing safety.

1. Identifying Worn Out Struts and Shocks

Before diving into the replacement procedure, it's essential to know when they need replacing. Telltale signs include:

- A notably rougher or bouncy ride.

- The vehicle "nose dives" when you apply the brakes.

- Uneven tire wear, indicating the tires aren't maintaining consistent contact with the road.

- Visible damage or leakages from the struts or shocks.

Ignoring these signs can compromise your vehicle's handling and increase stopping distances, particularly in emergency situations.

2. Preparing for the Job

Safety first! Before starting, ensure the car is on a level surface. It's advised to use safety stands to elevate the vehicle, providing clear access to the suspension components. Always wear safety gear, including gloves and safety glasses, to protect against any unforeseen mishaps.

3. The Replacement Procedure

After safely elevating your vehicle and ensuring you're equipped with the necessary tools, you can commence the replacement process:

a) Begin by removing the wheel, granting clear access to the suspension.

b) Identify the worn-out struts or shocks. While they might look similar, struts combine the spring and shock into a single unit, whereas shocks are standalone cylindrical components.

c) For **struts**: Attach spring compressors before unfastening any bolts. This safety step ensures the compressed energy in the spring is contained. Once safely secured, gradually loosen and remove the strut.

d) For **shocks**: Spot the securing bolts, and after loosening them, slide out the old shock.

e) Once the old components are out, install the new ones. Always refer to the manufacturer's instructions for any specific guidelines, ensuring an optimal fit.

f) After installation, inspect your work. Ensure there's no misalignment and all fastenings are secure.

4. The Importance of this Replacement

It cannot be stressed enough how vital struts and shocks are. They don't just contribute to a comfortable drive but are paramount to safety. Worn-out components can affect brake efficiency, tire health, and vehicle stability.

And as you close this chapter, proficiently equipped with the knowledge to replace struts and shocks, it paves the path to our next topic. In **Chapter 7**, we shall delve into the nuances of **Wheel Alignment and Tire Health**, further enhancing the safety and longevity of your vehicle. A well-aligned wheel not only ensures a straight drive but also plays a pivotal role in tire preservation. But more on that in the next chapter. Stay tuned!

Chapter 7: Wheel Alignment and Tire Health

Understanding Wheel Alignment

As you journey through the intricate world of automobile maintenance and mechanics, you'll come across the term **wheel alignment**. It might sound like a straightforward term, but understanding its deeper implications is essential for every car owner, from the newbie to the seasoned enthusiast.

Wheel alignment, at its core, refers to the adjustment of a vehicle's wheels so that they are parallel to each other and perpendicular to the ground. Imagine the wheels of a shopping cart, and you might recall a time when one wheel seemed to have a mind of its own, wobbling or veering off in a different direction. When this happens in a car, it can have significantly more severe implications than just a squeaky wheel.

One of the main reasons we emphasize the importance of wheel alignment is **safety**. Improperly aligned wheels can lead to erratic handling, especially when braking or during wet conditions. If the wheels aren't in harmony, the vehicle can pull to one side, requiring the driver to exert more effort and attention to keep the car straight. This can be taxing, and over long journeys, it might even become risky.

Apart from safety, let's delve into another critical aspect: **tire wear**. Tires are like the shoes of your vehicle; they experience wear and tear with every journey. However, if the wheels are misaligned, the tires can wear unevenly. One side might wear out faster than the other, leading to decreased tire life and a potential increase in running costs as you'd need replacements more frequently.

Lastly, there's an aspect of wheel alignment that might be particularly appealing to those conscious about their spending and the environment: **fuel efficiency**. Yes, something as seemingly trivial as the alignment of your wheels can impact how much fuel your car consumes. A misaligned vehicle has to work harder, which means it burns more fuel. Thus, ensuring your wheels are appropriately aligned can save you money at the pump and reduce your carbon footprint.

Now, you might be wondering how wheels get out of alignment in the first place. Various factors can contribute. From hitting a pothole at a particular angle to bumping a curb, or even regular wear and tear, all can knock your wheels out of their optimal alignment. It's why routine checks, especially after any notable jolts, are crucial.

In conclusion, wheel alignment isn't just a term thrown around in mechanic shops to sound technical. It's a fundamental aspect of car maintenance that touches on safety, the longevity of your tires, and even fuel economy. Remember, the journey of maintaining a vehicle isn't just about understanding complex components and jargon. It's about comprehending the symbiotic relationship between various parts and the holistic well-being of your ride.

Tools Needed for Alignment

Tackling wheel alignment in a DIY setting might sound challenging. However, with the right tools and some basic knowledge, it becomes a feasible endeavor for anyone keen on mastering their vehicle's maintenance. In this segment, we will explore the essential tools required for DIY wheel alignment, explaining their functions and importance in layman's terms. Keep in mind, though, while this guide covers the tools, executing the task requires patience and precision.

1. **Alignment Kit or Camber/Caster Gauge**: At the heart of the alignment process is the alignment kit. This tool measures the camber (tilt of the wheel from top to bottom) and caster (tilt of the steering axis when viewed from the side) angles of your vehicle's wheels. It's essential for ensuring your wheels are vertically aligned to the ground and that the steering axis is correctly positioned.

2. **Toe Plates**: These are flat plates, usually made of metal, that are placed in front of and behind the wheels. By using measuring tapes (which often come with the plates), you can measure the distance at the front and back of the plates, helping you determine the toe alignment. In simple terms, it helps you figure out if your wheels are pointed slightly inward or outward, which is crucial for straight-line stability.

3. **Steering Wheel Holder**: When aligning wheels, it's essential to ensure that the steering wheel remains stationary. A steering wheel holder keeps it in the dead center, allowing for more accurate adjustments to the wheels.

4. **Turn Plates**: These plates are vital when making adjustments to the caster. They sit beneath the tires, allowing you to rotate the wheels side to side without resistance, mimicking the movement of turning the steering wheel.

5. **Jack Stands**: Safety first! Whenever you're working under a vehicle or with its wheels, you must ensure the car is securely elevated. Jack stands are sturdy, triangle-shaped stands that hold the vehicle up, ensuring it doesn't fall during your alignment process.

6. **Digital Protractor or Angle Finder**: Especially useful for camber measurements, this tool helps in finding the exact tilt angle of your wheels. It ensures that the vertical tilt of your tires is within the manufacturer's specifications.

7. **Ruler or Straightedge**: Sometimes, the simplest tools are among the most crucial. A ruler or straightedge assists in making sure the toe plates are aligned correctly and can help verify other measurements.

8. **Chalk or Washable Marker**: Marking initial measurements and adjustments directly onto the tire or the ground can be incredibly helpful during the alignment process. It provides a clear reference point for any changes you make.

Having the right tools is only half the battle. As you gather these instruments, it's essential to become familiar with each one's functionality. Practice and patience will be your best allies in this endeavor. It's also worth noting that while DIY alignment can be gratifying, if you ever feel uncertain, there's no harm in consulting with a professional or seeking a second opinion.

In the vast world of automobile maintenance, wheel alignment stands out as a task that brings immediate, tangible benefits. It enhances the car's drive quality, increases tire lifespan, and improves fuel efficiency. As we transition into the next chapter, we'll delve deeper into another critical aspect of vehicle upkeep: **Tire Health and Maintenance**. From ensuring the right tire pressure to understanding wear patterns, it's all part of the journey to keep your vehicle running smoothly and safely.

How to Properly Align a Car's Wheels

Wheel alignment is fundamental to ensuring a vehicle's optimal performance. Misaligned wheels can lead to problems like uneven tire wear, a crooked steering wheel, or a vehicle that pulls to one side or another. This alignment process fine-tunes the angles of the wheels so they make consistent contact with the road. Below, we'll delve deeper into a more detailed DIY alignment, but remember, accurate measurements are crucial.

Step 1: Pre-Alignment Check

- **Inspection:** Begin by inspecting the car's **steering and suspension** components. Look out for worn out parts such as the **ball joints, tie rod ends**, and **bushings**. These components should be in top condition to ensure accurate alignment.

- **Replacement:** If damaged components are spotted, replace them. Wheel alignment on compromised parts won't yield accurate or lasting results.

Step 2: Car Positioning

- **Surface:** The car should be on a flat and level surface, essential for exact measurements. A garage floor or level driveway is ideal.

- **Brake:** Engage the parking brake for safety.

- **Wheel Centering:** Ensure the steering wheel remains centered throughout the process.

- **Turn Plates (Optional):** If available, place turn plates under the front wheels. They allow the wheels to turn without resistance, useful for caster measurements.

Step 3: Measure Current Alignment

- **Camber/Caster Gauge:** Use this tool to measure the current **camber** and **caster** angles of the wheels. These measurements should be noted and will act as your baseline.

- **Toe Plates:** Measure toe with toe plates. A pair of good quality measuring tapes can be helpful here. Standard settings often aim for a toe setting close to 0°, though slight toe-in (0.05° to 0.2°) is typical for many vehicles.

Step 4: Adjusting Camber

- **Understanding Camber:** Camber measures the vertical tilt of the wheels. Negative camber means the top of the tire is tilted inwards, and positive camber indicates it's tilted outwards. The exact measurement varies by vehicle, but a typical range is between -1° and 1°.

- **Adjustment:** To adjust camber, loosen the bolts on the upper or lower control arms or strut mounts, depending on your vehicle's suspension. Make small adjustments, then tighten and measure again.

Step 5: Adjusting Toe

- **Understanding Toe:** Toe refers to the angle at which the tires point relative to the centerline of the car. Measured in degrees or inches/mm, toe can be "in" or "out." A typical setting might be 1/16 inch (1.58 mm) toe-in.

- **Tie Rods:** Adjust toe by turning the tie rods. Loosen the locking nuts and turn the rod itself. Measure after each adjustment until the desired setting is achieved.

Step 6: Adjusting Caster

- **Understanding Caster:** Caster is the angle of the steering axis. Positive caster means the steering axis tilts toward the driver. For many cars, a typical caster setting is between 3° to 5° positive.

- **Adjustment:** Modifying caster often requires adjusting control arms. Depending on your car, this can be complex, so ensure you're comfortable before proceeding.

Step 7: Verification

- **Test Drive:** Take your car for a slow test drive in a controlled environment. The vehicle should not pull to one side, and the steering wheel should be centered. Recheck measurements after the drive to ensure everything held in place.

Step 8: Know When to Seek Professional Help

- **Measurement Accuracy:** Precision is paramount. If you cannot get accurate measurements or the vehicle doesn't feel right, consult a professional. Many shops have advanced alignment equipment that can provide a printout of all alignment angles.

Understanding the intricate details of wheel alignment is a mix of patience, precision, and practice. With proper alignment, not only is the ride smoother, but tires also last longer, saving time and money in the long run. As we transition to our next topic, we will explore the intricacies of **Tire Health and Maintenance**, ensuring a holistic approach to wheel care.

Chapter 8: Electrical Systems and Diagnostics

Basic Electrical Concepts

Automotive electrical systems, though intricate, can be broken down into comprehensible units, much like how an intricate watch can be understood by examining its individual gears and springs. At the heart of a vehicle's electrical system are three primary components: the **battery**, the **alternator**, and the **starter**. These three elements work cohesively, ensuring that your vehicle starts, runs smoothly, and powers all onboard electronics.

The **battery**, often recognized by its rectangular shape and two terminals, acts as the reservoir of electrical energy in your car. Think of it as the initial kickstarter. When your vehicle is off, it's the battery's job to provide the electrical current to the starter, and subsequently, to the rest of the car's electrical components. It ensures your radio, lights, or any other electronic device in your car, functions even when the engine is off. However, batteries don't last forever. Over time, they can lose their capacity to hold a charge. That's when you might experience the dreaded silent response after turning the key in the ignition.

Then we have the **alternator**. If the battery is the reservoir, the alternator is the replenisher. While the engine is running, the alternator ensures the battery remains charged and supplies additional power to the vehicle's electrical systems. Essentially, while the battery provides the initial spark to start the car, the alternator takes over once the engine is running, generating electricity and recharging the battery in the process. It's a continuous cycle of energy production and storage. A failing alternator might not recharge the battery effectively, leading to a situation where your battery is drained, and the vehicle won't start.

Last but not least, the **starter** plays a pivotal role. As its name implies, the starter's primary function is to start the engine. It takes the electrical charge from the battery and turns it into mechanical energy to turn the engine over. Imagine trying to push-start a heavy car down a hill to get the engine to turn over; the starter does a similar job but with electrical power. If the starter fails, the engine won't crank, no matter how healthy the battery or alternator might be.

While these components and their basic functions might seem straightforward, the vocabulary around automotive electrical systems can sometimes sound intimidating. Let's demystify some of these terms:

- **Voltage (V):** Think of this as the pressure of the electricity. A typical car battery has a voltage of around 12V, though some vehicles, especially hybrids, can have higher voltages.

- **Current (Amps, A):** This represents the flow of electricity, much like water flowing in a river. When you crank the starter, it draws a high current (often over 100A) from the battery.

- **Resistance (Ohms, Ω):** Resistance is what opposes or reduces the flow of electrical current. In some cases, resistance is useful (like in a bulb filament), while in others, unwanted resistance (like corrosion on a connector) can cause problems.

- **Circuit:** A complete path that allows electricity to flow. When you hear terms like "short circuit" or "open circuit," they refer to unwanted paths or interruptions in this flow, respectively.

In summary, the dance of electricity in your vehicle is a beautifully synchronized act, with each component playing its crucial part. Understanding these basics is the first step in diagnosing and addressing any electrical issues that might arise in your vehicle. As we delve deeper into automotive electrical systems in subsequent sections, you'll be better equipped to appreciate the intricacy and engineering marvel that goes into powering every flicker of light and turn of the engine in your car.

Using a Multimeter

One of the quintessential tools in the world of automotive diagnostics is the **multimeter**. A multimeter is akin to the Swiss army knife for anyone delving into electrical troubleshooting. This versatile instrument, often handheld, is designed to measure multiple electrical properties, including voltage, current, and resistance. For someone just starting, the myriad of dials, numbers, and probes on a multimeter can be a tad overwhelming. But, with a systematic approach, you'll soon find it's a lot simpler than it initially appears.

A multimeter's primary function is to help you determine what's going on within an electrical circuit. Is there a break in the wire (an open circuit)? Is there an unwanted connection (a short circuit)? Or perhaps you just want to know how much charge your battery holds? All these questions and more can be answered using this device.

Before diving into its usage, let's familiarize ourselves with a few essential parts of the multimeter:

1. **Display:** This is the digital or analog screen where your readings will appear.

2. **Dial/Selector Switch:** Used to select what you want to measure, such as voltage (V), current (A), or resistance (Ω).

3. **Probes:** Usually in red (positive) and black (negative), these are what you'll use to touch or connect to the parts you're testing.

Now, let's explore a step-by-step guide to utilizing this invaluable tool:

1. Setting up the Multimeter: Before making any measurements, ensure the multimeter is set correctly. Insert the probes into their respective ports—typically, the black probe goes into the common (COM) port, and the red one goes into the port labeled VΩmA or similar. Then, turn the dial to the desired measurement, like V for voltage.

2. Measuring Voltage: To measure voltage, such as testing a car battery, set the dial to 'DC voltage' (often represented by a V with a straight line). Connect the black probe to the battery's negative terminal and the red probe to the positive. A healthy, fully charged car battery should show around 12.6V.

3. Checking Resistance: If you suspect a broken wire or fuse, you'd measure resistance. Turn the dial to the Ω symbol. Touch the probes to both ends of the wire or fuse. A reading of '0' or close to '0' indicates good continuity, while a "1" or "OL" on a digital multimeter display denotes an open circuit.

4. Testing Current: For measuring current, it's a bit more involved as you need to measure the flow through the circuit. The dial should be set to the 'A' symbol. Remember, most multimeters can only handle low current values, so avoid measuring high current directly to prevent damage.

5. Interpretation and Troubleshooting: Learning to interpret readings is pivotal. For instance, if you're testing a light bulb filament for resistance and get an 'open circuit' reading, the bulb is likely blown. Similarly, a battery showing only 10V when tested might be discharged or failing.

Once you get a hang of the basics, it becomes a matter of practice. With every issue you diagnose and every reading you interpret, your proficiency will increase. Also, remember that while the multimeter is a potent diagnostic tool, sometimes the solution might lie in the simplest of places – like a loose connection or a blown fuse.

In the world of automotive diagnostics, understanding electrical readings is akin to a doctor interpreting vital signs. And just like a stethoscope for the doctor, the multimeter becomes an extension of your senses, letting you peer into the otherwise invisible realm of electrons and currents.

As we continue to dive deeper into the complexities of electrical systems, this foundational knowledge will pave the way for more advanced diagnostics. From sensors to intricate onboard computers, having a grasp on these basics ensures you're well-equipped to tackle challenges head-on.

Troubleshooting Electrical Issues

Beyond standard measurements, a multimeter can be a powerful tool in pinpointing a multitude of electrical issues in vehicles. Here's a comprehensive list of common problems and how you can utilize a multimeter to troubleshoot them:

1. Dead Battery:

- **Symptoms:** The car doesn't start, or electronics like lights and radio are weak or unresponsive.

- **How to Test:** Set your multimeter to DC voltage. Touch the black probe to the battery's negative terminal and the red probe to the positive. A reading less than 12.2V often indicates a dead or dying battery.

2. Bad Alternator:

- **Symptoms:** Battery warning light on, dimming lights when the engine is idling, or a dead battery despite recent charging.

- **How to Test:** Measure the battery voltage with the engine off and then with the engine running. The voltage should increase by 0.5 to 2V with the engine running if the alternator is charging.

3. Faulty Starter Motor:

- **Symptoms:** Car doesn't start, but lights and radio work. A clicking sound when the key is turned.

- **How to Test:** Set your multimeter to the resistance mode. Check the resistance of the starter solenoid by connecting the probes to its terminals. An infinite reading indicates a broken circuit inside.

4. Blown Fuses:

- **Symptoms:** Specific electrical components (like the radio or headlights) not working.

- **How to Test:** Switch the multimeter to continuity mode. Touch both fuse terminals with the probes. No reading means the fuse is blown.

5. Bad Ground Connection:

- **Symptoms:** Intermittent electrical issues, flickering lights, or components not working.

- **How to Test:** Use the resistance mode on your multimeter. Connect one probe to the ground connection point and the other to the battery's negative terminal. High resistance or no reading indicates a poor ground connection.

6. Malfunctioning Ignition Coil:

- **Symptoms:** Engine misfires or doesn't start.

- **How to Test:** Measure the resistance across the coil's terminals. If the reading is outside the manufacturer's specifications, the coil might be defective.

7. Poor Speaker Connection:

- **Symptoms:** Distorted audio or no sound from specific speakers.

- **How to Test:** Switch the multimeter to continuity mode. Check both ends of the speaker wire. If there's no continuity, there might be a break in the wire.

8. Defective Fuel Injector:

- **Symptoms:** Engine misfires or poor performance.

- **How to Test:** Measure the resistance across the injector's terminals. A reading outside the recommended range indicates a malfunctioning injector.

9. Faulty Sensor Wiring:

- **Symptoms:** Warning lights on the dashboard or abnormal engine behavior.

- **How to Test:** Set the multimeter to continuity mode and test the wires leading to the sensor. No continuity indicates a broken wire.

10. Inoperative Electric Window Motor:

- **Symptoms:** Power window doesn't move or moves slowly.

- **How to Test:** Check the voltage at the motor's terminals with the window switch pressed. If there's voltage but the motor isn't working, it may be defective.

While this list covers many common automotive electrical issues, it's by no means exhaustive. Cars are intricate machines with many interconnected systems. As such, it's crucial to approach each issue methodically and consider the broader system at play. When in doubt, always refer to the vehicle's service manual or seek professional advice. Remember, the multimeter is a guide, helping you make informed decisions, but a holistic understanding of the vehicle's systems will always serve you best.

Replacing Fuses and Relays

The modern car, with its intricate maze of electrical components, relies heavily on two seemingly small but pivotal elements: **fuses** and **relays**. When these components falter, the result can range from minor annoyances like a non-functioning radio to more severe issues like a car that won't start.

Firstly, let's dive into the concept of a **fuse**. Think of a fuse as a gatekeeper. It's a protective device that safeguards electrical circuits by preventing excess currents. Made of a metal wire or filament, it is housed inside a plastic body. When an electrical current is too strong – for instance, due to a short circuit – the wire inside the fuse heats up to its melting point and breaks, halting the current flow. This protects other vital components from getting damaged.

On the other hand, a **relay** is an electrical switch that opens or closes circuits by altering its physical state. It's like an electrical middleman, enabling small currents to activate larger ones. For instance, when you turn on your car's headlights, you're not sending power directly to them but instead triggering a relay which does the job for you.

Now, how does one identify and replace these components?

1. Identifying a Blown Fuse:

a. **Visual Check:** Modern cars often have a transparent plastic cover for their fuse boxes, allowing you to visibly inspect fuses. A blown fuse will show a broken or damaged filament.

b. **Multimeter Check:** As previously discussed, set your multimeter to the continuity setting. Touching the fuse's terminals with the probes will give a reading if the fuse is good. No reading? It's blown.

2. Replacing a Blown Fuse:

a. First, turn off the car and remove the key.

b. Open the fuse box, typically located under the dashboard or in the engine compartment. The car's manual will usually have a diagram indicating the position and purpose of each fuse.

c. Using a **fuse puller** or a pair of needle-nose pliers, gently remove the blown fuse.

d. Replace with a new fuse of the exact same amperage rating. Never use a higher amperage fuse as a substitute, as this poses a fire risk.

3. **Identifying and Replacing Faulty Relays:**

a. Symptoms of a faulty relay include devices or components that operate intermittently or not at all.

b. Locate the relay in question. This is often in the fuse box but can be elsewhere. Again, the car's manual is your guide.

c. Swap the suspect relay with another of the same type. If the component works with the swapped relay, then the original relay is faulty.

d. Replace with a new relay of the exact same type.

Understanding the signs of fuse and relay failures can save both time and money. Flickering lights, non-functioning components, or peculiar electrical behaviors can all hint towards these issues.

As you continue to enhance your knowledge and confidence in automotive diagnostics, remember that while today's cars are complex, they still adhere to foundational principles. The more you acquaint yourself with these basics, the better equipped you'll be to tackle more advanced challenges.

Speaking of advancements, the next chapter will plunge us into the world of the car's **Air Conditioning and Heating Systems**. How do they work? What happens when they falter? And most importantly, how can you ensure they keep you comfortable in any weather? Let's set our sights on that in the forthcoming section!

Chapter 9: Air Conditioning and Heating Systems

Understanding the AC System

The comfort of a cool breeze on a sweltering summer day, delivered directly from your car's dashboard, is something many of us might take for granted. Yet, behind that refreshing blast of cold air, lies an intricate system working tirelessly to keep you comfortable. Let's dive into the world of automotive **Air Conditioning (AC)** systems and demystify the magic behind it.

At its core, a car's AC system is a continuous loop of refrigerant that moves between gaseous and liquid states, absorbing and releasing heat in the process. This cycle involves a few primary components, each playing a pivotal role in cooling the air.

Compressor: Often dubbed the heart of the AC system, the **compressor** is a belt-driven device that compresses and circulates the refrigerant. As refrigerant enters in a gaseous state, the compressor pressurizes it, turning it into a high-pressure gas. This process is essential because the subsequent cooling occurs when this high-pressure gas releases its heat and changes back into a liquid form.

Condenser: The next stop for our high-pressure gas is the **condenser**, a component that might remind you of a small radiator. Situated at the front of the car, the condenser's job is to dissipate the heat absorbed by the refrigerant from the car's interior. As air from the car's movement or from the cooling fan passes over the condenser's fins, the refrigerant releases heat and condenses into a high-pressure liquid.

Receiver-Drier: Before the refrigerant can move to the next stage, any water vapor that may have entered the AC system needs to be removed. Enter the **receiver-drier**. This component acts as a filter, ensuring that only pure, moisture-free refrigerant reaches the next stage.

Expansion Valve: The high-pressure liquid refrigerant, now free from impurities, moves through the **expansion valve**. This valve acts as a tiny nozzle, allowing the refrigerant to expand and turn back into a gas. In doing so, its temperature drops dramatically, readying it to absorb heat from the car's interior.

Evaporator: Lastly, the refrigerant arrives at the **evaporator**, which sits inside the cabin. As the blower fan pushes warm interior air over the evaporator's cold fins, the refrigerant absorbs this heat and evaporates. This process cools the air, which is then directed into the car's cabin, delivering that refreshing breeze we all cherish.

This continuous transformation and flow of the refrigerant are regulated by a series of sensors and switches to ensure optimal performance.

Understanding the inner workings of your car's AC system not only fosters appreciation for the engineering behind it but also aids in troubleshooting should things go awry. Whether it's a lukewarm draft when you expected a chilly gust or an unusual noise from beneath the hood, a foundational knowledge empowers you to better communicate issues to professionals or even tackle minor problems yourself.

While the AC system cools us during the summer months, our cars also have a system to keep us warm during colder times. In the subsequent sections, we'll delve into the heating mechanisms that ensure our drives are just as comfortable in winter as they are in summer.

Recharging the AC System

Over time, an air conditioning system can lose its refrigerant or develop minor leaks, leading to a decrease in performance. If you've ever turned your car's AC on full blast during a hot day only to be met with mildly cool air, you might be in need of an AC recharge. Recharging, in layman's terms, involves topping up or replenishing the refrigerant in the system. While it may sound daunting, with the right equipment and guidance, you can tackle this task yourself. Here's a guide to safely and effectively recharging your car's air conditioning system.

Safety First!: Before beginning, remember that the **refrigerant** used in your car's AC system is under pressure and can be harmful if mishandled. Always wear safety goggles and gloves. Ensure you're working in a well-ventilated space and steer clear of open flames.

1. Gather Necessary Supplies:

- **AC Recharge Kit**: This is available at most auto parts stores and typically includes a pressure gauge, service valve, charging hose, and refrigerant.

- **AC Refrigerant**: Ensure you purchase the correct type, often denoted as R-134a for most cars produced after 1994.

- Safety goggles and gloves.

2. Prepare Your Car: Start your vehicle and turn the AC to the maximum. Let it run for a few minutes. This allows you to check the current performance before recharging.

3. Locate the Low-Side Service Port: This is where you'll connect the recharge kit. It's usually located on the larger diameter tubing between the compressor and the evaporator. The cap is often labeled with an "L".

4. Connect the Recharge Kit:

- Attach the charging hose of your kit to the can of **refrigerant**.

- Connect the other end of the hose to the low-side service port.

- Make sure connections are secure to avoid leaks.

5. Monitor the Pressure Gauge: Your kit's gauge will provide readings indicating the system's pressure. A color-coded scale often simplifies this:

- **Green**: Indicates adequate pressure.

- **Yellow**: Suggests it's slightly low and could benefit from a recharge.

- **Red**: Denotes a potential overcharge or a more severe issue that requires professional attention.

6. Add Refrigerant: If the gauge reads in the yellow zone:

- Open the valve on the recharge kit to allow the **refrigerant** to flow into the AC system.

- Regularly check the gauge to ensure it doesn't move into the red zone.

- Every minute, pause to check the AC's output inside the car. You're aiming for colder air.

7. Final Checks: Once satisfied with the coldness of the air, close the valve on the kit and disconnect it from the low-side port. Replace the port's cap. Let the car run for another few minutes to circulate the new refrigerant.

8. Dispose of Supplies: Never dispose of used refrigerant cans in regular trash. Check local regulations for proper disposal methods.

Tips:

- Overcharging the system can be harmful and decrease efficiency. Always monitor the pressure gauge closely.

- If your car consistently needs recharging, there may be a significant leak or another underlying issue. Seek professional help.

In conclusion, while the task of recharging your AC system might seem intricate, with patience and care, it's quite achievable. This newfound knowledge not only saves you a trip to the mechanic but also arms you with the understanding to maintain the comfort level inside your car, especially during those sweltering summer months.

Remember, though the AC system keeps us cool, the heating system is just as vital for those chilly mornings and frosty nights. Up next, we'll delve deeper into the complexities of the car's heating mechanisms, ensuring you stay cozy when the temperature drops.

Heater Core Replacement

As the chilly season approaches, the last thing any driver needs is a malfunctioning car heater. A car's heating system is indispensable for maintaining a comfortable cabin temperature, especially during cold weather. At the heart of this system lies the **heater core**, a vital component that operates much like a small radiator. If you've ever wondered why your vehicle's interior isn't warming up, or why the windows are getting foggy, a malfunctioning heater core might be the culprit. In this guide, we'll delve into the step-by-step process of replacing the heater core and highlight the symptoms of a failing one.

Understanding the Heater Core: The heater core is responsible for providing warm air into the vehicle's cabin. When you turn up the heat, coolant from the engine, which has absorbed heat, flows into the heater core. A fan then blows over the heated core, distributing warm air inside the car.

Symptoms of a Failing Heater Core:

1. **Cold Air**: One obvious symptom is when the heater only blows cold air, no matter how long the car has been running.

2. **Foggy Windows**: A leaking heater core can cause the interior windows to fog up due to the moisture it releases.

3. **Sweet Odor**: A distinct sweet smell inside the cabin is often indicative of a coolant leak, which could be from the heater core.

4. **Coolant Loss**: If you're consistently losing coolant and cannot find an external leak, it might be worth checking the heater core.

5. **Wet Passenger Floorboard**: If the heater core is leaking, coolant might find its way to the passenger side, dampening the floorboard.

Replacing the Heater Core:

Safety First: Always allow the car to cool down before starting any work. Coolant can be scalding when hot.

1. Disconnect the Battery: Begin by disconnecting the vehicle's battery. This ensures safety while working on internal components.

2. Drain the Coolant: Locate the drain valve on the radiator and drain the coolant into a container. Store it away safely, as it's toxic to animals and humans.

3. Access the Heater Core: This step can be a bit tricky. The heater core is usually located behind the dashboard on the passenger side. Depending on the vehicle model, you might need to remove the entire dashboard or just a section. Consult your vehicle's repair manual for specifics.

4. Disconnect Heater Hoses: Once the heater core is accessible, locate and disconnect the heater hoses. These are typically attached to the firewall in the engine compartment.

5. Remove the Old Heater Core: With hoses disconnected, you can now remove the heater core. It's generally held in place by brackets or screws.

6. Install the New Heater Core: Place the new heater core in the same position as the old one. Secure it using the brackets or screws you removed earlier.

7. Reconnect Heater Hoses and Dashboard: Reconnect the heater hoses to their respective ports. Once that's done, reassemble the dashboard.

8. Refill Coolant and Test: Refill the radiator with the coolant you drained or use new coolant if necessary. Reconnect the battery, start the car, and test the heating system.

If the heater works effectively, you've successfully replaced the heater core! It's a task that demands patience but offers immense satisfaction once completed.

In conclusion, ensuring your car's heating system functions optimally is essential not just for comfort but also for safety. With your newfound knowledge on heater cores, you're better equipped to tackle the challenges winter throws at your vehicle.

As our journey into vehicle maintenance continues, our next stop will delve into the echoes and rumbles of the car - the exhaust system. **Chapter 10: Exhaust System Maintenance and Repairs** will introduce you to the intricacies of this critical system, ensuring your car sounds just right and operates within environmental standards. Stay tuned!

Chapter 10: Exhaust System Maintenance and Repairs

Common Problems with the Exhaust System

As we transition from the comfort of our car's interior heating to the external rumbles beneath our vehicles, we're met with an often-underestimated component: the exhaust system. Designed to channel and expel the noxious gases generated by your vehicle, the exhaust system ensures that your car operates efficiently, safely, and with minimal environmental impact. But, like any other component, it's susceptible to a range of problems. In this section, we'll delve into some of the most **common issues** faced by exhaust systems, from the slow creep of rust to the unwelcome discovery of leaks and clogs. More importantly, we'll shed light on the risks of neglecting these issues.

1. Rust and Corrosion: Arguably the most common adversary of the exhaust system is **rust**. Originating from the constant exposure to water, both from the environment and as a byproduct of combustion, rust can weaken the metal components of the exhaust system over time. While surface rust might appear harmless, unchecked progression can lead to holes and subsequent leaks. If you live in areas where salt is used on the roads during winter or coastal regions with salt-laden air, the risk of rust is significantly heightened. Regular inspections and timely repairs can prolong the system's lifespan.

2. Exhaust Leaks: Identifying a leak in the exhaust system can be quite straightforward. An unusually loud rumble or a hissing sound is a giveaway. Leaks often result from rust, but they can also stem from cracked or damaged **gaskets** or due to the natural wear and tear of the exhaust components. Neglecting these leaks not only diminishes fuel efficiency but also poses health risks, as the escaping gases might find their way into the cabin, exposing occupants to harmful chemicals like carbon monoxide.

3. Clogged or Blocked Catalytic Converter: The **catalytic converter** is an essential part of the exhaust system, responsible for reducing harmful emissions. Over time, it can become clogged, especially if you're using low-quality fuel or oil, or if the engine isn't burning fuel completely. Symptoms include reduced acceleration, decreased fuel efficiency, or a sulfur-like smell. Ignoring a clogged converter can lead to reduced engine performance and can even cause engine overheating.

4. Damaged Exhaust Manifold: The **exhaust manifold** collects gases from multiple cylinders and funnels them into the exhaust pipe. Due to its location and function, it faces extreme heat and cold, making it susceptible to cracking or warping. A damaged manifold can result in engine performance issues and increased emissions.

5. Loose or Damaged Hangers: These are the parts that hold the exhaust system in place. Over time, **hangers** can wear out, leading to the system sagging or even detaching. Regular checks can ensure the exhaust stays where it should.

Risks of Neglecting Exhaust System Problems: While some exhaust issues might seem minor, neglecting them can escalate into more significant problems. Reduced fuel efficiency can be a drain on your wallet, while exposure to exhaust gases poses severe health risks. Additionally, a malfunctioning exhaust system impacts the environment, as it releases a higher amount of harmful emissions.

In essence, while the exhaust system might seem rugged and enduring, it isn't immune to wear and tear. Regular maintenance and prompt repairs can ensure it serves its purpose, keeping you, your car, and the environment safer.

How to Repair the Exhaust System

In the vast realm of automotive repair, the exhaust system may not be the most glamorous aspect to discuss, but it's undeniably one of the most vital. Without it functioning optimally, the performance, safety, and environmental-friendliness of your car are at risk. Having just navigated the common issues this system faces, let's dive into the hands-on realm of repairing some of these concerns. From the deep hum of the **muffler** to the intricate workings of **oxygen sensors** and **catalytic converters**, we will guide you through the steps of addressing the key components.

1. Replacing the Muffler: The muffler, as the name suggests, muffles the noise produced by the exhaust. A failing muffler can increase the noise level, and in some cases, it can also affect engine performance.

- **Step-by-Step Guide**:
    - First, ensure the vehicle is securely raised on jack stands. Remember, safety first.
    - Identify the **muffler clamps** that secure it to the exhaust system. These might be rusted, so some penetrating oil can help loosen them.
    - Using a wrench, remove these clamps. You might also need to remove hangers or rubber isolators, which can be done using a pry bar or pliers.
    - Slide the old muffler out.
    - Before installing the new muffler, inspect the exhaust pipe's condition. If it's rusted or damaged, consider replacing it.

- Slide the new muffler in place, secure it with the clamps, and ensure it's hanging at the right level with the hangers or isolators.

- Lower the vehicle and start the engine, checking for any unusual noises.

2. Replacing Oxygen Sensors: The **oxygen sensor** measures the amount of oxygen in the exhaust gases, providing feedback to the vehicle's computer to ensure optimal fuel combustion. A faulty sensor can decrease fuel efficiency and increase emissions.

- **Step-by-Step Guide**:

  - Disconnect the vehicle's battery.

  - Locate the oxygen sensor. Depending on the vehicle, there might be multiple sensors along the exhaust system.

  - Using an oxygen sensor socket or wrench, carefully unscrew the faulty sensor.

  - Install the new sensor by screwing it in place. Be cautious not to overtighten.

  - Reconnect it to the wiring harness and then reconnect the battery.

3. Replacing Catalytic Converters: The **catalytic converter** plays a vital role in reducing harmful emissions. Replacing one is a bit more involved but with the right tools and patience, it's manageable.

- **Step-by-Step Guide**:

  - Lift and securely support the vehicle on jack stands.

  - Spray the bolts holding the converter with penetrating oil to ease the removal process.

  - Using a wrench, remove the bolts on both ends of the catalytic converter.

  - Carefully remove the old converter.

  - Place the new converter in its position and bolt it securely.

  - Ensure everything is tightened and properly aligned.

  - Lower the vehicle and start the engine to check for any unusual sounds or exhaust leaks.

4. **Patching Small Exhaust Leaks**: Over time, the continuous heating and cooling of the exhaust system can result in minor holes and leaks. These small leaks, if left unaddressed, can lead to increased noise, reduced performance, and even potential carbon monoxide hazards. Here's a guide to patching those minor leaks.

- **Step-by-Step Guide**:

  - Start by safely raising your vehicle with jack stands to gain access to the exhaust system.

  - Locate the hole or leak in the system. A trick is to cover the end of the exhaust with a rag and listen for a hissing sound where the leak is.

  - Clean the area around the leak with a steel-toothed brush, removing any rust or debris.

  - For small holes, a heat-resistant epoxy can be applied. For larger holes, you might need an exhaust repair kit that comes with patches.

  - Apply the epoxy or patch as per the manufacturer's instructions. Ensure the exhaust is cold while working.

  - Allow the patch to dry and cure as recommended, usually several hours.

  - Lower the vehicle and start the engine, checking to ensure the leak has been sealed.

5. Repairing or Replacing Exhaust Hangers: The exhaust system is held in place under your vehicle by **exhaust hangers**. If they break or wear out, parts of the exhaust system can sag or come loose, leading to scraping sounds or potential damage.

- **Step-by-Step Guide**:

  - With the vehicle safely raised, inspect the entire length of the exhaust system, identifying any broken or worn-out hangers.

  - Using pliers or a suitable tool, remove the damaged hanger.

  - Position the new hanger in place and secure it. Ensure that the exhaust system is properly aligned and not sagging in any section.

  - Double-check the entire system to ensure all parts are securely held in place.

  - Lower the vehicle and give it a quick test drive to make sure there are no unusual sounds.

6. Replacing Exhaust Manifold Gasket: The **exhaust manifold gasket** seals the gap between the engine and the exhaust manifold, preventing exhaust leaks. If this gasket fails, you might hear a loud roaring noise from the front of the vehicle.

- **Step-by-Step Guide**:

  - Disconnect the battery and wait for the engine to cool down.

  - Remove any components blocking access to the exhaust manifold, such as heat shields.

- Using a wrench, carefully unscrew the bolts holding the exhaust manifold in place.

- Remove the old gasket and clean both surfaces (engine and manifold) thoroughly.

- Position the new gasket in place and reattach the exhaust manifold.

- Tighten the manifold bolts in a crisscross pattern to ensure even pressure.

- Reconnect any removed components and the battery.

- Start the vehicle and listen for any exhaust leaks, ensuring the gasket is sealed properly.

With these additional repairs under your belt, you'll be well-equipped to handle most common exhaust issues. These guides offer an overview of the process. Depending on the vehicle's make, model, and year, there might be slight variations As always, if a repair feels beyond your comfort level, consult with a professional.

Keeping the Exhaust System Clean

The exhaust system of a vehicle, although not often the topic of casual car conversations, holds paramount importance in ensuring smooth performance, reduced environmental footprint, and even the safety of the car's occupants. An optimally functioning exhaust system signifies a car that is running efficiently, produces minimal noise, and has a reduced emission of pollutants. Recognizing the significance of this system is the first step in its maintenance. Let's delve into the tips and strategies for maintaining a clean and efficient exhaust system, along with understanding the myriad benefits this upkeep offers.

Why Cleanliness Matters

Before we get our hands dirty with maintenance tips, we need to understand why cleanliness is crucial. At its core, the **exhaust system's primary role** is to manage and dispose of the combustion byproducts produced by the engine. These byproducts, when not channeled and processed appropriately, can degrade engine efficiency and contribute to environmental pollution.

1. **Environmental Consideration**: An exhaust system that is regularly maintained and cleaned ensures that the emission of pollutants such as hydrocarbons, carbon monoxide, and nitrogen oxides is minimized. As these pollutants contribute to smog, acid rain, and other environmental issues, keeping them in check is not only beneficial for your vehicle but also for Mother Nature.

2. **Performance Benefits**: A clogged or dirty exhaust can drastically reduce the performance of your vehicle. It can lead to decreased fuel efficiency, power loss, and even potential engine damage in severe cases. Keeping the exhaust system clean ensures that your car is always running at its peak potential.

Strategies for Maintaining a Clean Exhaust System

Now that we've understood the importance, let's focus on how to maintain it:

1. **Regular Inspection**: Start with a visual inspection. Look for signs of rust, cracks, or any visible damage. Listen for unusual noises when the car is running. A hissing or rattling noise could indicate a problem.

2. **Cleaning the Tailpipe**: Over time, the tailpipe can accumulate soot and other residues. Cleaning it regularly with a mixture of water and a cleaning solution can prevent buildup. For stubborn spots, a wire brush can be handy.

3. **Replace Rusting Components**: Rust is the nemesis of exhaust systems. If you identify any rusting sections during your inspection, consider replacing them. Rust can lead to holes in the exhaust, affecting performance and safety.

4. **Using Fuel Additives**: Some fuel additives can help reduce the buildup of carbon and other residues in the exhaust system. They can be added to your fuel and can help in keeping the system cleaner for longer.

5. **Professional Check-ups**: At least once a year, have your exhaust system checked by a professional. They can identify issues that might be missed during a regular inspection and can ensure that the system is functioning optimally.

In essence, the exhaust system, often out of sight and out of mind, plays a vital role in keeping our cars running smoothly and efficiently. Its maintenance might not always be on the top of our to-do lists, but recognizing its importance can make a significant difference in our driving experience and our environmental footprint.

As we conclude this chapter on exhaust systems, our journey into understanding our vehicles doesn't end here. In the upcoming chapter, **Chapter 11: Aesthetic and Functional Vehicle Care**, we will delve deeper into ensuring our vehicles are not just mechanically sound but also look and feel great. From the paint job to the interior fabrics, every aspect of a car's appearance impacts our driving experience. Stay with us as we transition from the mechanical world of exhausts to the world of aesthetics and functionality.

Chapter 11: Aesthetic and Functional Vehicle Care

How to Correctly Clean Your Vehicle and Leave No Scratch

Our vehicles, much like ourselves, benefit immensely from regular care and attention. Not only does this maintenance ensure longevity and optimal performance, but it also provides us with a sense of pride every time we hit the road. Arguably, one of the most visually satisfying aspects of this care regimen is a well-executed cleaning process. However, if done incorrectly, cleaning can inadvertently lead to unwanted scratches and damage to the car's surface. In this guide, we will delve deep into the art of vehicle cleaning, emphasizing techniques that safeguard the paint and finish.

The Importance of Gentle Cleaning

You might wonder why there's so much emphasis on 'gentle' cleaning. Cars are robust machines, right? While the machinery within is rugged, the vehicle's exterior finish is susceptible to micro-scratches and abrasions. A car's **paint** is its protective shield against environmental factors like UV rays, dirt, and pollutants. Any scratch, however minor, can compromise this defense, leading to further damage like paint chipping, fading, or corrosion.

Equipment and Products Matter

1. **Microfiber Cloths**: Always opt for **microfiber cloths**. Their unique structure allows them to pick up dirt and contaminants from the car's surface without causing any abrasions. They're vastly superior to regular rags or sponges in terms of both cleaning efficiency and safety.

2. **pH-Balanced Shampoos**: Not all cleaning agents are made equal. Using dish soap might seem like a handy alternative, but it's too abrasive for car paint. Instead, go for **pH-balanced car shampoos** that are specifically formulated to be gentle on your car's finish while effectively removing dirt.

3. **Two-Bucket Method**: This method involves using two buckets: one with soapy water and another with clean water. Dip the cloth into the soapy water, clean a section of the car, then rinse it in the clean water bucket. This prevents dirt from re-entering the soapy water, reducing the risk of scratches.

The Cleaning Process

Maintaining a car's external aesthetics goes beyond a mere wash; it's an art. Properly cleaning your vehicle ensures that its appearance remains pristine, and more importantly, that the integrity of the paint and finish remains uncompromised. Here's an expanded, in-depth guide to perfecting this process:

1. Preparation: Before you begin, ensure the car is parked in a shaded area. Direct sunlight can cause the soap to dry up quickly, leading to stains and spots. Also, make sure all windows and doors are properly closed to prevent water seepage.

2. Pre-rinse:

- Use a hose with a nozzle that allows control over the water's pressure.

- Start rinsing from the top, allowing the water to flow downwards. This helps dislodge the larger dirt particles and contaminants, ensuring they're rinsed off before the scrubbing begins.

- Pay extra attention to areas like wheel arches and under the bumpers, as these often accumulate more dirt.

3. Wheel Cleaning: Wheels are generally the dirtiest part of a car, collecting brake dust, road tar, and other contaminants.

- Use a **wheel cleaner** specifically designed for your type of wheels (aluminum, chrome, etc.).

- Use a separate microfiber cloth or a dedicated brush for the wheels to ensure contaminants don't transfer to the car's body.

4. Soaping:

- Dilute the **pH-balanced car shampoo** in one of your buckets as per the manufacturer's instructions.

- Submerge the microfiber cloth into the soapy water, ensuring it's completely soaked.

- Starting from the roof, apply the soapy water in a gentle, circular motion. Work in sections to ensure that each area gets adequate attention.

- As the cloth gets dirtier, rinse it in the second bucket with clean water before getting more soapy water. This **two-bucket method** ensures minimal dirt transfer, reducing the risk of scratches.

5. Rinsing and Drying:

- After the entire car is soaped, rinse it off, starting from the top and working your way down.

- For drying, avoid letting the car air-dry as this can cause water spots. Instead, use a clean, dry microfiber cloth. Employ a patting motion rather than dragging the cloth across the surface to avoid any potential scratches.

- Ensure areas like door jams, behind mirrors, and other nooks and crannies are also dried, as leftover water can cause rust or mold over time.

6. Claying (Optional, but recommended): Over time, contaminants can embed themselves into the paint, causing a rough feel. A **clay bar** can help remove these, ensuring a smooth surface.

- After lubricating the surface with a clay lubricant, gently glide the clay bar over the car's surface. The clay will pick up embedded contaminants.

- Keep reshaping and checking the clay; when it gets too dirty, it should be replaced.

7. Finishing Touches: Once the car is dried, applying a **wax** or **sealant** can offer both a protective layer and a noticeable shine. Using a soft foam applicator, apply the wax in a thin layer, working in sections. Allow it to haze, then buff off with a clean microfiber cloth.

Remember, cleaning your vehicle isn't just about aesthetics; it's a ritual that preserves the integrity of the car's finish, ensuring a prolonged lifespan and sustained value. With the right technique, products, and a bit of patience, every cleaning session can leave your car looking as immaculate as the day it rolled out of the showroom. While we've just scratched the surface (pun intended) of vehicle care, mastering the cleaning process is an essential step in the comprehensive journey of maintaining your car's aesthetics and functionality.

Interior Cleaning and Detailing: Breathing New Life into Your Vehicle's Inner Sanctum

The interior of your car is a sanctuary. It's where you spend countless hours, whether you're commuting, traveling, or simply reflecting during a quiet moment. Over time, the inside of a vehicle can become a collector of crumbs, dirt, stains, and even some unwelcome odors. Much like the external body of the car, the interior too requires a structured cleaning process to keep it looking and smelling fresh.

Materials for Interior Cleaning and Detailing

1. Basic Cleaning Tools:

- **Car Vacuum Cleaner:** Preferably one with various attachments to reach crevices, under seats, and tight spots.

- **Microfiber Cloths:** Soft, lint-free, and perfect for cleaning and polishing without scratching surfaces.

- **Soft-Bristled Detailing Brush:** For dusting vents, intricate designs, and tight spaces.

2. Dashboard and Central Console Care:

- **Interior Detailing Solution:** Ensure it's suitable for your car's dashboard material, such as leather, vinyl, or plastic.

- **Soft-Bristled Brush:** Useful for getting into the small crevices and intricate designs of the dashboard and controls.

3. Seat and Upholstery Cleaning:

- **Fabric Cleaner:** Suitable for fabric seats to tackle stains and spills.

- **Leather Cleaner and Conditioner:** If your car has leather seats, this dual-action product helps clean and maintain the leather's suppleness.

- **Soft-Bristle Brush:** For scrubbing stubborn stains on fabric seats.

4. Window and Windshield Care:

- **Automotive Glass Cleaner:** Specifically designed for vehicle windows, ensuring no residue or streaking.

- **Paper Towels or Window Microfiber Cloths:** Essential for a streak-free finish.

-

5. Carpet and Floor Mat Revitalization:

- **Carpet Cleaner Spray or Foam:** For tackling stains and ground-in dirt.

- **Stiff-Bristled Brush:** Useful for agitating carpet fibers to lift stubborn dirt.

- **Soap:** Mild detergent for cleaning rubber mats.

6. Odor Control:

- **Car Fresheners:** For quick freshness boosts, available in various forms like hanging cards, gel cans, or vent sticks.

- **Car Odor Eliminator:** A more permanent solution, these products target and neutralize odor-causing molecules.

7. Miscellaneous:

- **Plastic Bags or Trash Bags:** For collecting trash and debris during the decluttering phase.

- **Buckets:** Useful if you decide to mix your cleaning solutions or for holding water when cleaning mats.

- **Gloves:** To protect your hands from chemicals, especially if you have sensitive skin.

Having the right materials at your disposal ensures that the cleaning process is efficient, effective, and safe for both the car and the person doing the cleaning. Always remember to check the manufacturer's recommendations or read the label before applying any product to ensure compatibility with your vehicle's materials.

Here's how you can systematically breathe new life into your car's inner spaces:

1. De-clutter and Preliminary Cleaning: Before diving deep into detailing, remove any items that don't belong in the car. Toss out trash, remove miscellaneous items, and clear the storage pockets. Vacuuming is the next essential step. Using a **car vacuum cleaner**, ensure you reach under the seats, the gaps between seats, and all the small crevices. Pay special attention to the footwells and trunk area.

2. Dashboard and Central Console: The dashboard and central console are the most visible parts of your car's interior. They also tend to accumulate dust quickly.

- Begin by dusting with a microfiber cloth to remove the loose particles.

- Use an **interior detailing solution** suitable for your car's material (be it leather, vinyl, or plastic). Spray the solution onto the cloth, not directly onto the surface, to avoid oversaturation.

- Gently wipe down the dashboard, steering wheel, infotainment system, and other associated areas. Ensure you navigate around buttons and knobs delicately.

- For tight areas or intricate designs, a soft-bristled detailing brush can be handy.

3. Seats and Upholstery: Seats often bear the brunt of spills, stains, and wear.

- Begin by vacuuming the seats to remove any crumbs or loose dirt.

- For fabric seats, a **fabric cleaner** can do wonders. Spray the cleaner on the stained areas and gently scrub with a soft-bristle brush. Wipe away with a clean cloth and let it dry.

- For leather seats, utilize a **leather cleaner and conditioner**. This not only cleans but also keeps the leather supple, preventing cracks.

- Once done, if possible, leave the doors open to let the seats air out and dry naturally.

4. Windows and Windshields: Although seemingly straightforward, clean windows can significantly enhance the driving experience.

- Using an **automotive glass cleaner**, spray onto a cloth or directly onto the window. Wipe in an up-and-down motion followed by side-to-side to ensure no streaks are left behind.

- Clean the inside of the windshield from the passenger side to avoid contorting awkwardly over the steering wheel.

5. Carpets and Floor Mats: Ground-in dirt, spills, and heel marks are standard issues here.

- Start by removing the mats and giving them a good shake.

- Vacuum the car floor and mats diligently.

- Use a **carpet cleaner** for any stains. A brush can help agitate and lift stubborn dirt.

- For rubber mats, a rinse with water, followed by scrubbing with soap and drying, should suffice.

6. Eliminating Odors: Last but not least, address the smells that might have built up over time.

- For a quick fix, **car fresheners** are available. However, for long-lasting freshness, consider using a **car odor eliminator**. These products target odor-causing molecules, neutralizing them rather than merely masking the smell.

By devoting time to clean and detail the interior of your vehicle, not only do you enhance its aesthetic appeal, but you also create a healthier and more pleasant environment for every journey. A rejuvenated interior can make even an old car feel brand new, providing comfort and pride in your cherished possession. Remember, it's not just about the destination, but the joy and serenity of the journey - and a pristine interior plays a significant role in that experience.

How to Repair Rust on Your Car Without Welding

The persistence of rust on cars, often referred to as the 'cancer' of vehicles, can significantly deteriorate a car's aesthetics and functionality. Addressing it early, especially before it corrodes through the metal, is paramount. Thankfully, you can remedy early-stage rust without advanced welding techniques. This guide offers an in-depth exploration of how to confront and restore rust-damaged areas using non-welding techniques.

1. Assessment and Identification

Understanding the severity of rust on your vehicle is your first port of call. There are primarily three rust stages:

- **Surface rust:** This type only affects the top layer of paint. It's manifested by small brown spots or patches.

- **Scale rust:** Ignoring surface rust can escalate to this level. Here, rust begins to affect the metal's integrity underneath the paint.

- **Penetrating rust:** The most severe form, this rust type eats into the metal, creating holes and jeopardizing structural integrity.

This guide targets surface and scale rust. However, if you observe penetrating rust, it might necessitate advanced techniques or professional intervention.

2. Gather Essential Materials

Ready your workspace with the following:

- **Safety Goggles and Gloves:** Essential gear to shield your eyes and hands from particles and chemicals.

- **Rust Converter:** A specialized solution that chemically transforms rust into a paint-ready, stable substance.

- **Sandpaper (from 60 to 2000 grit):** A range is vital because different rust stages and subsequent steps require varying grits.

- **Primer, Paint, Clear Coat:** Aim for shades that mirror your vehicle's original hue.

- **Clean Cloth and Mild Soap:** These assist in cleaning away residues.

- **Painter's Tape and Newspaper:** Imperative for shielding unaffected areas from accidental paint or primer touches.

3. Preparing the Rusty Area

Safety first: gear up with your gloves and goggles. Commence with the coarsest (60 or 80 grit) sandpaper. Sand the rusted region, focusing on eradicating the rust and exposing the bare metal beneath. Progressively switch to finer sandpapers to attain a smooth, even surface, ensuring all rust particles have been dealt with. Post-sanding, wash the area gently using the cloth and mild soap to eliminate any residue. This step ensures an uncontaminated base for the upcoming processes.

4. Rust Converter Application

With a dry and cleaned area, it's time to introduce the **rust converter**. This chemical marvel halts any underlying rusting process by stabilizing the iron oxide (rust) into a substance that's less prone to rusting again. Adhering to the converter's label directions, uniformly coat the rusted area. Ensure it sits and dries as prescribed, typically a few hours or overnight for optimal results.

5. Priming and Painting

Post rust converter application, it's time to reintroduce color. First, safeguard the surrounding, unaffected car sections with painter's tape and newspaper. Initiate with a thin **primer** coat, allowing it to dry fully. The primer acts as a foundation, ensuring paint adherence and longevity. Afterward, methodically layer on your car's paint, ensuring each coat dries entirely before introducing the next. Two to three layers usually yield the best results, providing rich color while masking any repair signs.

6. Finishing Touches

With the paint set, the **clear coat** comes into play. This transparent layer acts as a protective shield against external elements like UV rays, which could fade the paint over time. Moreover, it gives your car that desired shiny finish. Apply it uniformly and let it dry for several hours.

Pat yourself on the back! Your vehicle should now flaunt a rejuvenated spot, devoid of any rust traces. This DIY approach not only saves dollars but also instills a sense of accomplishment.

In sum, while these techniques effectively address minor to moderate rust occurrences, substantial damages might require expert attention. Vehicles, much like any other asset, benefit immensely from timely care and attention.

As we segue into the intricacies of car care, our upcoming chapter takes you under the hood. Gear up to understand the nuances of **Engine and Performance Tuning** to unleash your vehicle's true potential.

How to Remove Scratches from Car PERMANENTLY

A scratch on your car, irrespective of how minimal, can be an agonizing sight. The good news is, most of these scratches can be treated, restoring your vehicle's pristine appearance. To achieve this, it's essential first to understand the nature of the scratch, as not all scratches are equal. Let's delve into this and provide you with effective methods to bid adieu to these unwanted scars permanently.

Understanding the Depth of a Scratch

The depth of a scratch largely dictates its removal approach. Your car's exterior has multiple layers: the **clear coat, paint layer, primer**, and then the **metal panel**. Scratches can affect any of these layers, with each depth requiring a distinct repair method:

1. **Clear Coat Scratch:** The most superficial scratch type, affecting only the protective clear coat.

2. **Paint Scratch:** A deeper scratch penetrating the clear coat and reaching the paint beneath.

3. **Primer Scratch:** More severe, this scratch affects the primer layer, just above the metal.

4. **Deep Scratch:** The gravest type, affecting the metal panel itself.

Materials Required

To address these scratches, you'll need:

- **Rubbing Compound:** Helps level the clear coat surrounding the scratch.

- **Polishing Compound:** Restores the shine after using the rubbing compound.

- **Sandpaper (2000 and 3000 grit):** For wet sanding the affected area.

- **Clear Coat Spray:** To restore the protective layer after deeper repairs.

- **Microfiber Cloth:** For applying compounds and general cleaning.

- **Touch-up Paint Kit:** Necessary for paint and primer scratches.

- **Soap and Water:** For cleaning the affected area before the process.

Treating the Scratch

Effective treatment of car scratches hinges on the correct approach suited to the scratch type. Let's delve deeper into each of the methods previously outlined to provide you with an even clearer picture:

For Clear Coat Scratches: Superficial scratches that merely affect the clear coat are the easiest to manage, but attention to detail remains essential:

1. **Cleaning:** *First, clean the affected area with a mix of soap and water, ensuring no dirt or debris remains that could further damage the surface. Thoroughly dry the area with a microfiber cloth.*

2. **Applying Rubbing Compound:** *With a separate, clean microfiber cloth, apply a coin-sized amount of the **rubbing compound**. Using circular motions, gently buff over the scratch. This compound works as a very fine abrasive, smoothing out the clear coat around the scratch. Buff until you notice the scratch diminishing.*

3. **Residue Removal:** *Once you're satisfied with the buffing, use a fresh cloth to wipe away any residue.*

4. **Polishing:** *Apply a dollop of the **polishing compound** to another clean cloth. Gently work the compound over the treated area in circular motions, restoring the lost shine.*

5. **Final Clean-Up:** *Wash the area one more time to remove any leftover compound, ensuring a seamless finish.*

For Paint Scratches: These are more challenging due to the depth but can be remedied with patience:

1. **Cleaning:** *Wash the affected region with soap and water, ensuring it's free from dirt. Dry thoroughly.*

2. **Touch-Up Paint:** *Using a touch-up paint kit that matches your car's exact shade, carefully apply the paint over the scratch using steady, even strokes. Let it dry as per the manufacturer's recommendation, which is typically several hours.*

3. **Leveling the Surface:** *You may notice a slight elevation or unevenness where the paint was applied. To address this, wet the 2000 grit sandpaper slightly and gently sand the area to level it. Always sand in the direction of the scratch for best results.*

4. **Refinement:** *Following the initial sanding, use the 3000 grit sandpaper for a smoother finish.*

5. **Shining:** *Once you're satisfied with the surface, apply both the **rubbing and polishing compounds** as detailed in the clear coat scratch section.*

For Primer and Deep Scratches: *Such scratches can be daunting but are treatable with due diligence:*

1. **Thorough Cleaning:** *The deeper the scratch, the more essential the cleaning. Ensure the area is devoid of any contaminants.*

2. **Touch-Up Paint Application:** *As with the paint scratch, use a touch-up kit to cover the scratch. Ensure even application and let it dry thoroughly.*

3. **Sanding for Evenness:** *Begin with the 2000 grit sandpaper, wetting it slightly. Sand the painted area gently to level any unevenness. Transition to the 3000 grit sandpaper for a finer finish, ensuring the area blends seamlessly with the surrounding surface.*

4. **Clear Coat Restoration:** *Once satisfied with the sanded area, spray the **clear coat spray** to restore the protective layer. Allow it to dry according to the product's instructions.*

5. **Finishing Touch:** *Conclude by applying the **rubbing compound** followed by the **polishing compound** to reintroduce the shine, ensuring the treated area is indistinguishable from the surrounding surface.*

Remember, the key to effective scratch treatment is patience, ensuring each step is performed meticulously. While the steps outlined can remedy most scratches, deeply penetrated ones or those near edges might require professional attention.

Maintaining the Restored Surface

Post-scratch removal, it's pivotal to maintain the treated area. Regularly wash and apply a car wax or sealant, which acts as a barrier against potential scratches and provides a glossy finish.

In essence, while scratches might seem like a perpetual nuisance, knowing their nature and having the right tools at hand can empower you to restore your car's immaculate appearance. While superficial scratches are manageable by most car owners, deeper ones might require more patience and finesse. And if in doubt, never hesitate to consult a professional.

How to Repair Car Headlight Broken Lens

The headlights of a vehicle play an indispensable role in nighttime driving, ensuring both the driver's and pedestrians' safety. One component of the headlight that often faces wear and tear is the **lens**. Over time, the lens can become cloudy due to oxidation or, worse, suffer cracks or breaks from minor accidents or debris. When such an incident occurs, it's crucial to address the problem promptly, as a compromised lens can reduce light output, diminish visibility, and even let in moisture, leading to further complications. Fortunately, if a replacement is not immediately possible or desired, a broken lens can be temporarily fixed. This chapter provides a practical guide on how to repair a broken headlight lens effectively.

Understanding the Damage

Before diving into the repair, it's essential to assess the damage. Minor cracks may only require sealing, while more significant breaks could necessitate additional attention. The goal is to restore as much clarity as possible while preventing further damage and moisture entry.

Materials Required

Before starting, ensure you have the following tools and materials:

1. **Clear Tape or Lens Repair Film**: Ideal for temporary repairs to prevent moisture ingress and further damage.

2. **Silicone Sealant**: Helps in sealing minor cracks and providing a waterproof barrier.

3. **Sandpaper (600, 1000, and 2000 grit)**: For smoothing out the edges of the break and preparing the surface.

4. **Plastic Adhesive**: For more significant breaks, to bind parts of the lens together.

5. **Clean Cloth & Isopropyl Alcohol**: To clean the area before applying any adhesive or sealant.

The Repair Process

Undoubtedly, the repair process for a headlight lens involves meticulous attention to ensure effective results. While the initial overview provides a basic understanding, diving deeper into the procedure can further aid those seeking detailed guidance.

1. **Cleaning the Area**: This step is foundational for a successful repair. Thoroughly cleaning the lens with isopropyl alcohol ensures the surface is grease-free. Using a soft cloth, apply the alcohol in a circular motion, concentrating more on the damaged parts. Allow the lens to air dry for a few

minutes post-cleaning. A clean surface ensures better adhesion and prevents contaminants from getting trapped during the repair.

2. **Sealing Minor Cracks**:

   - **Application**: With a small nozzle or fine-tipped tool, apply a steady, thin bead of silicone sealant directly into the crack. Ensure that the sealant penetrates well, filling the entire crack.

   - **Smoothing**: Using a flat-edged tool or spatula, gently smooth out the sealant so it's flush with the lens's surface. This not only ensures a more discreet repair but also reduces light diffusion.

   - **Curing**: Allow the sealant to cure according to the manufacturer's instructions. During this period, avoid any water contact or harsh conditions.

3. **Addressing Bigger Breaks**:

   - **Preparation**: Begin by sanding the edges of the broken pieces using the 600-grit sandpaper. This roughens the surface slightly, promoting better adhesion.

   - **Alignment**: Before applying adhesive, do a dry run. Ensure you know how the broken pieces fit together, reducing the chance of mistakes when using the adhesive.

   - **Adhesive Application**: Using a brush or applicator, apply a generous amount of plastic adhesive to the sanded areas. While being liberal, avoid excessive application to prevent overflow or messy finishes.

   - **Binding**: Carefully align the broken lens pieces, pressing them together firmly. Secure them in place using tape if necessary. Let the adhesive set for the time recommended by its manufacturer.

4. **Finishing**:

   - **Initial Sanding**: Once the adhesive has dried, start by sanding the repaired area using 1000-grit sandpaper. This removes excess adhesive and smoothens the surface.

   - **Fine Sanding**: Transition to the 2000-grit sandpaper, further refining and smoothing the repair area, ensuring a seamless blend with the surrounding lens.

   - **Cleaning**: Wipe down the area with a clean cloth, removing any sanding residue.

   - **Protection**: Consider applying a clear UV-resistant sealant over the entire lens. This not only protects the repair but also acts as a preventive measure against future oxidation.

5. **Temporary Measures**: For immediate measures, clear tape or lens repair film offers a quick solution. Ensure the lens is dry and free from dust. Cut the tape or film to size and apply it over the damage. Smooth it out to prevent air bubbles, ensuring a tight seal against moisture and dirt.

Remember, while these procedures can offer significant improvement and a temporary solution, if the damage continues to compromise the lens's integrity, consult a professional or consider a full headlight unit replacement.

Navigating challenges with our vehicles doesn't just stop with physical repairs. As we shift our focus from the aesthetics and functional care of our vehicles, it's time to equip ourselves with knowledge for those unexpected situations on the road. Our next chapter, **Handling Emergency Situations**, is a deep dive into preparing every driver for the unforeseen.

Chapter 12: Handling Emergency Situations

Creating an Emergency Kit for Your Vehicle

Emergencies are unpredictable and can happen even to the most cautious drivers. Equipping your car with a comprehensive emergency kit is not merely a suggestion—it's a necessity. Let's delve deeper into each essential item in your kit and why they are indispensable.

1. **First Aid Kit**: Accidents, no matter how minor, can cause injuries. A well-stocked first aid kit can be pivotal in such circumstances. Make sure it includes items like band-aids, antiseptic wipes, adhesive tape, gauze pads, tweezers, scissors, pain relievers, cotton balls, and a detailed first-aid manual. This kit can serve to treat minor wounds or to provide temporary relief until professional help arrives.

2. **Jumper Cables**: Batteries can be temperamental and die without warning. Quality jumper cables, preferably those that are at least 10 feet long and coated with 8-gauge rubber, can be connected to another vehicle to jump-start your car. It's a temporary solution, allowing you to drive to the nearest service station for a proper assessment.

3. **Flashlight with Extra Batteries**: A durable, waterproof flashlight can be invaluable if you find yourself stranded during nighttime. LED flashlights are recommended due to their longevity and brightness. Always store it with extra batteries or consider a hand-crank version that doesn't rely on batteries.

4. **Flares or Reflective Triangles**: To alert other vehicles of your presence during a breakdown, especially during the night or in low visibility conditions, use brightly colored flares or reflective triangles. Position them at a distance from your vehicle to give incoming drivers ample reaction time.

5. **Fire Extinguisher**: While rare, vehicle fires can be catastrophic. A compact fire extinguisher designed specifically for automotive use can combat small fires, potentially saving lives and the vehicle itself. Ensure it's rated for Class B (flammable liquids like gasoline, oil) and Class C (electrical fires).

6. **Multi-Tool or Basic Toolkit**: A robust multi-tool or a basic toolkit should be durable and rust-resistant. Essential components would be screwdrivers (both Phillips and flathead), pliers, an adjustable wrench, a cutter, a small knife, and perhaps a set of hex keys. These tools can facilitate minor fixes, from tightening a loose screw to cutting a frayed wire.

7. **Tire Repair Kit and Pump**: Tires are susceptible to punctures. A tire repair kit, complete with tire sealant and a tire plugger, offers a temporary solution. Accompany this with a portable air compressor that can inflate your tire, giving you enough time to reach the nearest garage.

8. **Water and Non-perishable Food Items**: If you're stranded for a prolonged period, especially in remote areas, staying hydrated and fed becomes critical. Store a few bottles of water and non-perishable food items, such as energy bars, nuts, or dried fruits, that can provide essential nutrients.

9. **Blanket**: A thermal or fleece blanket is essential, especially in colder regions. If you're stranded in the cold and the car's heating system fails, a blanket can be a lifesaver, preventing hypothermia.

10. **Charged Cell Phone and Charger**: Communication is key in emergencies. A fully charged cell phone, preferably with a car charger or a portable power bank, ensures you can call for assistance. Consider also storing emergency numbers, including local tow services and roadside assistance.

11. **Local Maps**: Digital navigation is useful but may be unreliable in areas with poor cell reception. A detailed local map or a road atlas can be invaluable in such situations. Familiarize yourself with the major routes and landmarks to ensure you can navigate even when technology fails.

Building a comprehensive emergency kit might seem extensive, but remember, it's always better to have it and not need it than to need it and not have it.

Drawing a close to our discussions on **Handling Emergency Situations**, always remember that prevention and preparedness go hand in hand. Next, we'll dive into **Understanding Your Vehicle's Electronics** in Chapter 12, highlighting the intricate fusion of mechanics and cutting-edge electronics that modern vehicles represent.

What to Do in Case of a Breakdown

The moment you sense something is wrong with your vehicle, your heart might race, and a plethora of thoughts can cloud your judgment. It's a situation no one wants to find themselves in, but being well-prepared can make all the difference.

Here's a detailed guide on how to handle a vehicle breakdown:

1. Stay Calm and Evaluate: It's natural to feel a surge of panic. Take a moment to breathe deeply, which will help calm your nerves and think more clearly. As you do, try to pinpoint any unusual symptoms your car is exhibiting. This could be anything from sudden vibrations, a drop in power, odd noises, or unfamiliar warning lights illuminating on the dashboard. Recognizing the issue, whether it's as blatant as a blown tire or more subtle like diminishing engine performance, can guide your subsequent actions.

2. Switch on Your Hazard Lights: The immediate step after noticing a problem, even before you pull over, is to activate your **hazard lights**. These blinking orange lights are universally recognized and alert other drivers that you're facing an issue, prompting them to give you space and reduce their speed around your vehicle.

3. Safely Move to the Side: The goal here is to get out of the flow of traffic swiftly but safely. Keep your movements smooth and predictable; avoid any abrupt maneuvers. If you're on a multi-lane road, signal and move to the farthest right lane first, then gradually make your way to the shoulder. If you're near an exit, it might be more beneficial to take it and then find a safe spot to park.

4. Exit the Vehicle Safely: If the surroundings permit and you deem it safe, get out of the vehicle—but always use the door that's furthest from traffic. On highways or busy streets, it's sometimes safer to remain inside the vehicle. If you do stay inside, keep your seatbelt on, as it offers protection should another vehicle accidentally collide with yours.

5. Call for Help: After ensuring safety, it's time to summon assistance. If you're subscribed to a **roadside assistance** program, now's the time to use it. Be ready to provide them with your location, a brief description of the issue, and any other pertinent information. If you aren't a member of such a service, calling a local mechanic or tow service is the next best option.

6. Stay with Your Vehicle: As you wait for help, it's advisable to stay close to your vehicle, especially if you're in a remote area. Being present makes it easier for the rescue team or tow truck to spot you. However, always prioritize your safety—if the environment seems unsafe due to weather, location, or any other factor, seek shelter but ensure it's within a visible range from your car.

7. Set Up Warning Signals: If you've packed **reflective triangles** or flares in your emergency kit, now's the time to use them. Place them at varying distances behind your car, starting from about 10 feet and going up to 50 feet. If it's foggy or visibility is hampered, ensuring you're seen from a distance becomes even more crucial.

8. Document Everything: While waiting, take the time to document the state of your vehicle. Snap a few photos, especially if there's visible damage. These can be invaluable for insurance claims or diagnostics later on. If any witnesses stop to help or offer insights, it might be useful to note down their accounts too.

9. Avoid Attempting Major Repairs: The roadside is not an ideal workshop. Even if you have some technical know-how, delving deep into repairs can be dangerous due to passing traffic and the unpredictability of the issue at hand. Minor issues like changing a tire or topping up water can be done, but anything more complex should be left for a safer environment and professional tools.

10. Prepare for the Unexpected: Every breakdown is a lesson. Once resolved, reflect upon it. Maybe it highlights the need for a regular maintenance check, or perhaps you found gaps in your emergency preparedness. Taking these lessons on board ensures you're better equipped for any future mishaps.

Handling a car breakdown can be daunting, especially if it's your first experience. However, with the right knowledge, mindset, and tools, you can make the ordeal less stressful and ensure safety for yourself and others on the road.

Changing a Flat Tire

A flat tire can be a motorist's worst nightmare, especially if you find yourself stranded in an unfamiliar area. Yet, with the right tools and understanding, changing a tire can be a straightforward task. Here's a comprehensive guide to getting you back on the road without unnecessary stress.

Recognizing the Problem: Often, a flat tire announces itself with a sudden drop in vehicle stability, a thudding sound, or a steering pull. If you suspect you have a flat, reduce your speed gradually and look for a safe, flat place to pull over. It might be a parking lot, a service area, or the side of a well-lit road.

Safety First: Before you start, make sure you're parked far from the traffic and on a solid, level surface to prevent the car from rolling. Turn on your **hazard lights**, especially if it's dark or visibility is poor due to weather.

Tools and Preparations: For this task, you'll need a few essential tools:

1. **Jack:** This device lifts the car off the ground, allowing you to remove the flat tire and replace it.

2. **Lug wrench:** A special wrench designed to remove the lug nuts from your wheel.

3. **Spare tire:** Always ensure your spare is properly inflated and in good condition.

4. **Wheel chocks or heavy stones:** To place behind the opposite tire to prevent rolling.

Loosening the Lug Nuts: Using the lug wrench, start by slightly loosening each lug nut. Don't fully remove them yet; just break the initial tightness. It's easier to do this while the tire is still on the ground, as it prevents the wheel from spinning.

Lifting the Vehicle: Position the jack under the car's designated jacking point. These are typically found near the wheel well and are reinforced to support the car's weight. As you pump or turn the jack, ensure it remains steady and straight. Lift the vehicle until the flat tire is a few inches off the ground.

Removing the Flat Tire: Now, fully unscrew and remove the loosened lug nuts. With both hands, grasp the tire and pull it towards you. If it's stuck, a gentle side-to-side wiggle should free it.

Installing the Spare Tire: Align the spare tire with the lug nut bolts, then push it into place. It's crucial to ensure the tire is seated flat against the hub. Hand-tighten the lug nuts as much as you can.

Lowering the Vehicle: Carefully lower the vehicle using the jack, ensuring it descends smoothly and straight. Once the vehicle is fully on the ground, use the lug wrench to tighten the lug nuts in a crisscross pattern. This ensures even pressure and prevents warping.

Final Checks: Inspect the spare tire to ensure it's fully seated, and the lug nuts are secure. Store all your tools and the flat tire in your vehicle. Remember, the spare is a temporary solution. Plan to visit a mechanic soon to inspect the tire and potentially get a replacement.

In the vast landscape of vehicle maintenance, knowing how to change a tire is a fundamental skill. It not only provides independence but can also save time and money.

As you grow in your car ownership journey, it's essential to familiarize yourself with various aspects beyond just emergency situations. Next, we'll delve into **Chapter 13: Navigating Car Ownership and Repair Costs.** This chapter will demystify costs associated with car ownership, helping you budget wisely and recognize when you're being overcharged.

Chapter 13: Navigating Car Ownership and Repair Costs

Understanding the Costs of Ownership

Driving conjures up images of freedom, open roads, and spontaneous adventures. However, beneath the allure of the open road lies a mesh of financial obligations that extend far beyond the car's price tag. Let's delve into these costs, offering insights on average prices and invaluable advice to help you navigate car ownership's financial labyrinth.

Initial Purchase Price: This is your starting point. New cars can range from $20,000 for basic models to upwards of $70,000 for luxury brands. Used cars, available at dealerships, private sales, or online platforms like CarMax and AutoTrader, can vary widely based on age, model, and condition, typically starting from $5,000. It's advisable to conduct thorough research and perhaps even have a trusted mechanic inspect a used vehicle before purchase.

Insurance: A non-negotiable recurring cost. On average, American drivers spend between $800 and $1,500 annually on **car insurance**. Factors influencing this include the car's make, your age, and driving history. Providers like GEICO, Progressive, and State Farm offer comparative rates. Always review and compare policies, and consider bundling with home insurance for potential discounts.

Registration and Licensing: Annual **registration** fees in the U.S. generally range from $20 to $200, varying by state and vehicle type. Remember, some states also impose taxes during registration. And don't forget the cost of renewing your driver's license, which typically ranges between $30 and $90 every few years, dependent on the state.

Fuel: The U.S. national average hovers around $3 to $4 per gallon for gasoline, though this fluctuates. If you drive 15,000 miles annually and your car averages 25 miles per gallon, expect to spend about $1,800 to $2,400 yearly on fuel alone. Apps like GasBuddy can help you find the best local gas prices.

Maintenance: Essential for longevity and safety. On average, expect annual costs of $500 to $700 for routine **maintenance**. Dealerships, local garages, and chain stores like Jiffy Lube or Firestone offer these services. It's beneficial to maintain a consistent service schedule and keep all receipts for future reference or resale value.

Repairs: Unexpected and occasionally pricey. Setting aside a contingency of around $1,000 annually can buffer against unexpected repairs. Using reputable mechanics, sourced from recommendations or platforms like Yelp, can ensure quality work and prevent future issues.

Depreciation: Cars, especially new ones, can lose 20%-30% of their value in the first year. By year five, this can soar to 60% or more. If you're considering resale, keep this in mind. Certified pre-owned cars can offer a balance between value and reassurance, as they've already faced the steepest part of their **depreciation** curve.

Taxes: In states like Virginia or Missouri, you might be charged an annual **property tax** on your vehicle, which can be several hundred dollars. Other states might levy a one-time tax at purchase or mandate an annual fee based on your car's value.

Parking and Tolls: City dwellers may face daily parking fees of $10 to $40 or monthly rates exceeding $200. Regularly using toll roads can add up to $100 or more monthly. Apps like ParkWhiz or Waze can guide you to affordable parking and toll-free routes.

In closing, while cars symbolize freedom, they come with a price tag that extends beyond the showroom. By grasping these costs, you can budget judiciously, ensuring your car doesn't become a financial burden. Making informed decisions at every stage will ensure a smoother ride, both on the road and in managing your finances.

Finding and Working with a Professional Mechanic

Car ownership, while liberating, often demands dealing with technical challenges that require the assistance of a professional mechanic. The relationship you build with your mechanic is essential. A reliable mechanic not only saves you money but also ensures your vehicle's longevity and your safety on the road. The following are insightful steps and advice on locating and fostering a fruitful relationship with a trustworthy mechanic.

1. Start with Recommendations: One of the most tried-and-true methods of finding a reliable mechanic is through word of mouth. Ask friends, family, or coworkers about their experiences. A mechanic that comes highly recommended by someone you trust is often a safe bet. Remember, the most sizable advertisements don't always correlate to the best service.

2. Research Online Platforms: Platforms such as Yelp, Google Reviews, and the Better Business Bureau can provide **peer reviews** that shed light on a mechanic's reputation. While no business is immune to the occasional negative review, a pattern of complaints is a red flag.

3. Check for Certifications: A trustworthy mechanic shop will often display their **certifications** prominently. Look for affiliations with the National Institute for Automotive Service Excellence (ASE) or similar reputable organizations in your country. These certifications are proof of the mechanic's expertise and ongoing training.

4. Ask the Right Questions: When you approach a mechanic, be clear about your concerns and listen to their diagnostic approach. A good mechanic will explain issues in layman's terms and provide a clear cost estimate. Don't be shy; ask questions about parts, labor, warranties, and any potential additional costs.

5. Start Small: Before committing to major repairs, start with a small job like an oil change or tire rotation. This initial experience will give you a sense of their professionalism, efficiency, and customer service.

6. Transparency is Key: A reputable mechanic will be transparent about their findings. They should be willing to show you the damaged or worn parts, explaining why replacements are necessary. Additionally, upon request, they should provide the old parts for your inspection, a practice that demonstrates honesty.

7. Be Wary of Constant Upsells: While mechanics might suggest preventive measures or point out potential issues, be cautious if they consistently push for additional expensive services. An honest mechanic will prioritize essential repairs and explain the urgency of each.

8. Maintain Open Communication: As with any professional relationship, open communication is paramount. Ensure you provide a reachable contact number and request updates if the repair is extensive or taking longer than anticipated.

9. Keep Records: Always ask for a detailed invoice outlining the work done, parts replaced, and their respective costs. This **documentation** is not only essential for warranty claims but also beneficial if you decide to sell the car in the future.

10. Build a Relationship: Once you find a mechanic you trust, stick with them. A mechanic that is familiar with your car's history can offer better-tailored advice, anticipate potential issues, and ensure your vehicle receives consistent care.

In conclusion, finding and working with a mechanic is an integral aspect of car ownership. The journey might seem daunting, but with thorough research, clear communication, and a little patience, you can foster a professional relationship that will serve you and your vehicle well for years to come.

Communicating Effectively with Auto Professionals

Owning a vehicle can sometimes feel like a commitment, much like maintaining any long-term relationship. Central to this commitment is the need for open and effective communication, especially with those who understand its intricate details – the auto professionals. Discussing your car's needs with a mechanic is an art in its own right. Proper communication can mean the difference between accurate diagnostics and unnecessary repairs. Let's delve into how you can best prepare for these conversations and ensure your vehicle gets the care it requires.

1. Familiarize Yourself with the Basics: While you don't need to be a car expert, having a general understanding of **auto terminologies** and basic car parts can significantly improve the clarity of your conversations. For instance, know the difference between terms like transmission and drivetrain, or brake pads versus brake rotors. This base knowledge will empower you to ask pertinent questions and comprehend the explanations provided.

2. Be Specific about Symptoms: "It's making a weird noise" is not as descriptive as "There's a high-pitched squeal when I start the car in the morning." The more precise you can be about the symptoms and conditions under which they appear, the easier it will be for the mechanic to diagnose the issue.

3. Mention Any Recent Repairs or Changes: If your car recently had work done or if you noticed the issues shortly after a particular event (like an accident or after hitting a pothole), inform the mechanic. This context can provide valuable clues.

4. Don't Hesitate to Ask Questions: It's your right as a car owner to understand what work is being done on your vehicle. If a term is unfamiliar or if you're unsure about a recommended service, ask. Queries like "What is the function of that part?" or "How does this issue affect my car's performance?" are entirely valid.

5. Request a Walk-through: If possible, ask the mechanic to show you the problem. Visual explanations can often clarify complex issues. For instance, seeing a worn-out brake pad next to a new one can provide a clearer understanding of why a replacement is necessary.

6. Be Open but Cautious: While it's essential to trust the expertise of auto professionals, it's equally vital to be an informed consumer. If a suggested repair seems excessive or unnecessary, consider seeking a **second opinion**. It's not about doubting the mechanic, but ensuring you're making the best decisions for your car and wallet.

7. Clarify Costs Upfront: Before any work begins, ensure you have a clear estimate that breaks down parts, labor, and any additional fees. It's okay to ask for clarification on any line items that seem ambiguous.

8. Stay Accessible: Provide a reliable contact method, be it your phone number or email. If a mechanic discovers an additional issue while working on the car, they should be able to reach you promptly to discuss further actions.

9. Offer Feedback: After the service, share your experience. Constructive feedback can help mechanics improve their service, and positive feedback can bolster their reputation.

10. Foster Mutual Respect: Remember that mechanics are skilled professionals. Treating them with the same respect you'd give to any other professional can go a long way in building a lasting and fruitful relationship.

In sum, effective communication with your mechanic is foundational in ensuring your vehicle gets optimal care. While the technicalities of auto repair can sometimes feel overwhelming, a well-informed conversation can demystify the process. As you navigate through the maze of car ownership and its associated challenges, remember that clear dialogue is a beacon.

As we transition from understanding the nuances of car ownership and repair costs, the journey takes us to another pivotal aspect of vehicular responsibility. Chapter 14 delves into the "Legal and Environmental Considerations" surrounding cars, casting light on the broader implications of being a car owner in today's world.

Chapter 14: Legal and Environmental Considerations

Handling and Disposing of Chemicals

In the vast world of automotive care, maintenance isn't just about keeping your vehicle running smoothly. It's also about being a responsible car owner, and this responsibility extends far beyond safe driving. Vehicles, as intricate machines, are reliant on numerous chemicals, many of which are harmful to both humans and the environment if not handled correctly. Grasping the how and why of safe chemical disposal is not just a legal requirement; it's a moral imperative for the conservation of our planet.

1. Automotive Fluids - The Basics: Every vehicle houses multiple types of fluids - oil, brake fluid, coolant, transmission fluid, to name a few. These are vital for its performance and safety. However, over time, these fluids degrade and require replacement. What many don't realize is that the disposal of these old fluids is not as simple as pouring them down a drain or into the soil. Such actions can lead to environmental damage and, consequently, legal repercussions.

2. The Environmental Impact: Why all the fuss about a bit of used oil or coolant? Well, these **automotive fluids** often contain heavy metals and other toxins. When introduced into the environment, they can contaminate soil and groundwater. This not only affects plant and animal life but can also find its way into our drinking water, posing health risks.

3. Local Disposal Facilities: Every locality usually has designated centers or facilities for disposing of hazardous materials. It's advisable to familiarize yourself with the nearest such facility. These centers have specialized equipment and protocols to ensure that automotive fluids are disposed of without harming the environment.

4. Oil Changes: One of the most frequently replaced fluids is motor oil. While changing oil, using a sealed container to catch the old oil can prevent spills. Many auto stores and local disposal facilities offer **oil recycling**, ensuring it gets refined and reused rather than causing environmental harm.

5. Antifreeze (Coolant) Awareness: Despite its vibrant color, antifreeze is particularly harmful. It's toxic to humans and animals even in small quantities. Always store antifreeze in sealed containers away from children and pets. When it's time for disposal, never mix antifreeze with other fluids. Specialized recycling centers handle antifreeze, transforming it into a reusable product.

6. Brake and Transmission Fluids: Due to the heavy metals and toxins they contain, these fluids also require special care. While they can sometimes be disposed of similarly to motor oil, always confirm with the recycling facility regarding their specific requirements.

7. Batteries: While not a fluid, car batteries contain acid and other harmful materials. They should never be dumped with regular trash. Instead, bring them to battery recycling facilities where they can be safely processed and the metals within them salvaged.

8. Be Prepared for Spills: Despite our best efforts, accidents can happen. Having an **absorbent material** like cat litter or sand on hand can help manage and clean up spills. Remember, immediately cleaning up reduces the environmental impact and keeps your workspace safe.

9. Stay Informed and Updated: Environmental and disposal regulations can evolve. It's wise to periodically check with local environmental agencies or related bodies to remain compliant with current guidelines.

10. Educate and Advocate: Being responsible doesn't stop at personal actions. Educate friends and family about the importance of proper chemical disposal. By fostering awareness, the collective effort can lead to a significant positive impact on our environment.

In summary, as auto enthusiasts or even just responsible car owners, our duties go beyond mere vehicular maintenance. By understanding and practicing safe and legal methods of disposing of automotive chemicals, we actively contribute to a healthier environment. It's a testament that being mechanically inclined and environmentally conscious aren't mutually exclusive; they harmoniously coexist in the realm of responsible car ownership.

Legal Restrictions on DIY Auto Work

The world of automotive DIY is incredibly rewarding, offering not just an opportunity to understand and bond with your vehicle but also to save on maintenance costs. However, there's an essential caveat for the enthusiastic home mechanic: not everything is permitted under the law. This doesn't mean that governments are against you keeping your car in tip-top shape. Rather, these legal stipulations are in place to ensure safety, environmental responsibility, and fair economic practices.

1. **Why Restrictions Exist:** Before diving into the specifics, let's understand the *why* behind these restrictions. The primary reason for these legal boundaries is **public safety**. Vehicles are complex machines, and mistakes in critical systems can pose severe risks to the driver, passengers, and others on the road. Environmental concerns also play a significant role. Incorrectly disposed chemicals or emissions from improperly modified vehicles can damage our environment. Lastly, there are economic implications. Unlicensed businesses or individuals offering professional services can have repercussions on the economy and lead to unfair business practices.

2. **Emissions and Environmental Laws:** One of the main areas where DIY enthusiasts need to be careful is emissions. Many regions have strict regulations on vehicular emissions to combat air pollution. Modifying your exhaust system or removing the catalytic converter, for instance, might make your car sound more powerful, but it's illegal in many places due to the increased pollution it causes. Before making such changes, always consult local emissions guidelines or even consider getting an emissions test done post-modification.

3. **Safety Components:** Brakes, seat belts, airbags - these are all critical safety components in a car. While routine maintenance like brake pad replacements can be done at home, overhauls or modifications to these systems are often regulated. For instance, disabling an airbag system or modifying seat belts might seem like a good idea for a racing modification, but doing so can render your vehicle illegal for road use.

4. **Structural Changes:** Modifying the structural integrity of a vehicle is a gray area in DIY automotive work. Cutting into the chassis, for instance, to fit larger tires or to modify the car's stance, can affect its safety in the event of a collision. Many jurisdictions require inspections for structurally modified vehicles to ensure they adhere to safety standards.

5. **Unlicensed Sales and Services:** If you've honed your skills and want to make a bit of money on the side, be wary. Offering automotive repair services without the proper licenses is illegal in many regions. This ensures that those working on vehicles have the necessary training and adhere to professional standards.

6. **Stay Educated:** Rules and regulations change. If you're passionate about DIY auto work, regularly check your local and national regulations. Joining an automotive club or online forum can be beneficial as members often share updates and insights related to legal considerations.

7. **When in Doubt, Seek Professional Advice:** It's always a good idea to consult professionals when unsure about a modification or repair, especially if it seems to be in a legal gray area. They can provide advice, ensuring you stay compliant with the law, and more importantly, keep your vehicle safe for use.

In summary, DIY auto work is a fulfilling hobby and, for many, a necessity. But with this freedom comes responsibility. Always prioritize safety, environmental health, and legal adherence. The open road welcomes the well-informed and responsible DIY enthusiast, ensuring a harmonious blend of passion and responsibility.

Certification for Handling Refrigerants

The vehicle you drive is a marvel of modern engineering, filled with complex systems that work in harmony to provide you with a comfortable and safe journey. One such system, the air-conditioning (AC) system, ensures your comfort during those hot summer days. Central to the AC system's operation is a substance called a **refrigerant**. While vital for cooling your vehicle, refrigerants can be hazardous if mishandled. This leads us to the importance of certifications for those working with automotive refrigerants.

1. **The Role of Refrigerants:** At its core, the refrigerant is a substance used in the AC system to absorb and release heat, which helps cool the inside of your vehicle. However, the release of refrigerants into the atmosphere can have detrimental effects on the environment. Some refrigerants, especially older types, can deplete the ozone layer, while others act as potent greenhouse gases.

2. **Why Certification Matters:** Given the environmental concerns, there are strict regulations governing the handling, recovery, and recycling of refrigerants. The certification isn't just a piece of paper; it's an assurance that the individual understands the risks associated with refrigerants and knows how to manage them properly. Incorrect handling can lead to refrigerant leaks, which can be harmful to the environment and costly for the vehicle owner.

3. **Getting Certified:** If you're keen on DIY car maintenance or considering a professional path in automotive repair, it's crucial to be certified if you plan to work with refrigerants. In many regions, it's illegal to purchase refrigerants without certification. Certification programs usually cover topics like the properties of refrigerants, proper techniques for recovery, recycling, and charging, and the environmental impact of refrigerants. Most programs end with an examination to ensure understanding.

4. **How to Obtain Certification:** The exact process varies by region, but typically, an individual would need to enroll in a recognized training program. These programs can be found at technical schools, community colleges, or through automotive organizations. After completing the training, you'll need to pass a certification exam. Once certified, you'll be legally allowed to purchase and handle automotive refrigerants.

5. **Maintaining and Updating Your Certification:** Just like with other technical fields, the world of automotive refrigerants is ever-evolving. Newer, more environmentally-friendly refrigerants are being developed, and techniques for handling them are refined. It's essential to keep updated with these changes. Certification bodies often require periodic re-certification or continuous learning credits to ensure professionals stay informed.

6. **For the Enthusiastic DIYer:** While it might seem tempting to top off your vehicle's refrigerant or fix a minor leak, remember that the risks—both legal and environmental—are significant. If you're not certified, it's always best to consult with a professional when it comes to your vehicle's AC system. They have the knowledge, tools, and certification to ensure the job is done correctly and safely.

In wrapping up, the world of automotive maintenance and repair is vast, with various facets requiring specific knowledge and skills. As you delve deeper into understanding your vehicle, always prioritize safety, the environment, and legal guidelines. And as we journey forward into the next chapter, we'll explore strategies to **Save Money on Parts and Supplies** without compromising on quality and reliability.

Chapter 15: Saving Money on Parts and Supplies

Where to Shop: Finding Quality Auto Parts on a Budget

When it comes to auto maintenance and repair, the cost of parts and supplies can quickly add up. Whether you're a DIY enthusiast looking to perform your own repairs or simply someone keen on ensuring your vehicle gets the best, understanding where to source quality parts without overspending is essential. This guide aims to shed light on where you can find reliable auto parts that won't empty your wallet.

1. Local Auto Parts Stores: The first and most obvious place many people turn to is their local **auto parts store**. These brick-and-mortar establishments offer the advantage of immediate availability. You can inspect parts firsthand, ensuring they're the correct fit for your vehicle. Many also have knowledgeable staff who can offer advice. However, prices can sometimes be higher due to overhead costs. *Tip:* Build a relationship with your local store. Regular customers often get discounts or are informed about ongoing sales.

2. Chain Retailers: Bigger chains such as AutoZone, O'Reilly, and Advance Auto Parts often have more comprehensive inventories and might offer price matching. Their purchasing power can sometimes translate to better deals for consumers. They also often provide online catalogs, making it easy to check availability before you drive down.

3. Online Marketplaces: Websites like Amazon, eBay, and RockAuto have become go-to places for auto parts shoppers. These platforms offer a wide variety of brands and often at competitive prices. The **downside** is that you can't physically inspect the product before purchase, and shipping times can vary. *Tip:* Always check seller reviews and ratings. Ensure they're reputable and have good feedback from previous buyers.

4. Direct from Manufacturer: If you're particular about getting OEM (Original Equipment Manufacturer) parts, consider purchasing directly from the manufacturer's website or authorized dealer. While this may sometimes be more expensive, you're assured of the part's authenticity and fit.

5. Junkyards and Salvage Yards: Don't underestimate the treasures you might find in a **junkyard** or salvage yard. While the parts are used, you can often find components in good condition for a fraction of the price of a new one. It's especially useful for older vehicles where parts might be discontinued. However, you must know what you're looking for and be ready to inspect parts thoroughly.

6. Swap Meets and Car Shows: These events can be goldmines for hard-to-find parts. Enthusiasts often gather, bringing along parts they no longer need. While it's a bit of a wild card, you might just find that rare piece you've been searching for.

7. Online Forums and Social Media Groups: Joining car forums or social media groups dedicated to your specific vehicle make or model can be enlightening. Members often sell parts or can direct you to trusted sellers. Plus, the shared experience can provide insights into which brands or parts are more reliable or offer better performance.

In conclusion, the world of auto parts shopping offers a myriad of options, each with its pros and cons. It's crucial to balance cost with quality and reliability. Remember, the cheapest option isn't always the best in the long run. Prioritize the safety and performance of your vehicle, and don't hesitate to seek advice or do thorough research before making a purchase. With the right knowledge and resources, ensuring your vehicle runs smoothly without overspending is entirely within reach.

New vs. Used Parts: Weighing Your Options for Vehicle Maintenance

As a car owner, whether you're engaging in a DIY repair project or simply sourcing parts for a mechanic, the question often arises: should you buy new or used parts? Each choice comes with its distinct advantages and challenges. Let's delve into the pros and cons of both new and used parts to help you make an informed decision for your vehicle's needs.

New Parts: The Fresh Choice

Advantages:

1. **Reliability:** One of the foremost benefits of new parts is the peace of mind you get from their reliability. These components haven't experienced wear and tear, ensuring optimal performance straight out of the box.

2. **Warranty:** New parts often come with a manufacturer's **warranty**. This guarantees replacement or repair if the part fails within a specific period, providing an added layer of financial security.

3. **Compatibility:** Sourcing a new part specifically designed for your vehicle's make and model ensures a perfect fit and optimal performance.

4. **No History of Damage:** New parts have no history of damage or misuse, reducing the risk of early failure.

Disadvantages:

1. **Cost:** New parts are typically more expensive than their used counterparts. For those on a tight budget, this can be a significant consideration.

2. **Availability:** For older car models, finding new parts can be challenging. Manufacturers may discontinue certain components after a number of years, making them harder to locate.

Used Parts: The Economical Alternative

Advantages:

1. **Cost-Efficiency:** The primary allure of used parts is their cost-effectiveness. You can often obtain them for a fraction of the price of new components, making them an attractive option for budget-conscious individuals.

2. **Eco-Friendly:** By opting for used parts, you contribute to reducing the environmental impact. Reusing parts means less waste and fewer resources used in manufacturing.

3. **Availability:** Older or rare car models may benefit more from used parts, especially when new ones are not in production anymore.

Disadvantages:

1. **Potential Wear and Tear:** The most evident drawback of used parts is their history. They've been in a working vehicle before, which means they've experienced some level of wear. This could impact their lifespan and performance.

2. **Uncertain History:** It's hard to know the exact history of a used part. It could've been in an accident or exposed to unfavorable conditions, which can affect its functionality.

3. **Limited or No Warranty:** Used parts might come with a shorter warranty period or none at all, potentially leading to higher costs if they fail soon after installation.

In making your decision, consider the nature of the repair. For critical components that influence safety – like brake systems or steering mechanisms – it's often advisable to lean towards new parts due to their reliability. On the other hand, for less crucial components or if you're restoring an older model where authenticity is a priority, used parts might be more appropriate.

Lastly, always prioritize quality. Whether you're choosing new or used parts, ensure you're sourcing from reputable suppliers or dealers. Do your research, seek reviews, and possibly consult with a trusted mechanic. Your vehicle's longevity, performance, and safety hinge on the parts it's equipped with, so making informed choices is paramount.

OEM vs. Aftermarket Parts: Making the Right Choice for Your Vehicle

In the vast world of automotive parts, two terms that frequently pop up are **OEM** and **aftermarket parts**. Both these categories play crucial roles in the auto industry, and understanding their nuances can significantly influence the performance, aesthetics, and cost-efficiency of your vehicle repairs and upgrades.

Here's a breakdown of the differences between the two and some insights to guide your decision-making process.

OEM Parts: The Original Components

OEM, or **Original Equipment Manufacturer**, parts are components produced by the very same manufacturer that made parts for the automaker. In simple terms, if you purchase an OEM part for your Ford Mustang, that component is made by the manufacturer that Ford used for the original parts.

Advantages of OEM Parts:

1. **Guaranteed Fit:** Since OEM parts are made by the same manufacturer, they're guaranteed to fit perfectly. There's no guesswork involved.

2. **Consistency:** With OEM, the quality remains consistent. You're getting the same part that came with your vehicle, which often means top-notch durability and performance.

3. **Warranty Assurance:** Most OEM parts come with a warranty, ensuring you get repairs or replacements if there's an issue.

Drawbacks of OEM Parts:

1. **Higher Cost:** OEM parts typically cost more than their aftermarket counterparts. This can be especially challenging if you're working with a limited budget.

2. **Limited Availability:** Not all retailers stock OEM parts. You might have to head to a dealership or a specialized store, which could be less convenient.

Aftermarket Parts: The Alternative Route

Aftermarket parts are components made by companies other than the original equipment manufacturer. After buying your car, if you decide to get a part that isn't from the car's original maker, that's an aftermarket part.

Advantages of Aftermarket Parts:

1. **Cost-Efficiency:** Often, aftermarket parts are less expensive than OEM parts. This price difference doesn't necessarily indicate inferior quality; it's just a different market.

2. **Variety:** The aftermarket industry offers a broader range of parts, from performance-enhancing components to aesthetic modifications.

3. **Availability:** Aftermarket parts are widely available at various retailers, auto shops, and online platforms.

Drawbacks of Aftermarket Parts:

1. **Overwhelming Options:** The vast array of choices in the aftermarket scene can be confusing, especially for beginners. It can be tough to determine which brands are reputable.

2. **Quality Variability:** While many aftermarket parts match or even surpass OEM quality, others might not meet the standards. Research and reviews become crucial.

3. **Potential Warranty Issues:** Some car manufacturers might void warranties if you install aftermarket parts, so it's essential to check beforehand.

In making your decision between OEM and aftermarket, consider the following:

- **Purpose:** Is it a critical repair, or are you looking for an upgrade?

- **Budget:** Determine what you're willing to spend and see which option provides the best value.

- **Vehicle's Age:** Older models might benefit more from aftermarket parts, especially if OEM parts are hard to find.

To conclude, the choice between OEM and aftermarket parts revolves around individual needs, budget constraints, and personal preferences. While OEM offers consistency and guaranteed compatibility, the aftermarket provides variety and cost-effectiveness. No matter the route you take, always prioritize quality and informed decision-making.

As we transition from the intricacies of parts and supplies, our journey takes us to the realm of continuous learning. In Chapter 16, "Continuing Education and Resources," we delve into the importance of staying updated in the ever-evolving automotive world, ensuring your skills remain sharp and your knowledge ever-expanding.

Chapter 16: Continuing Education and Resources

Staying Current with Automotive Trends: Navigating the Fast-paced World of Automotive Evolution

The automotive industry is not static. Like most technological domains, it's in perpetual motion, constantly pushing the boundaries of innovation and design. For enthusiasts, mechanics, and anyone deeply involved with cars, staying abreast of these rapid changes isn't just a luxury; it's essential. This continuous evolution offers not only a more profound appreciation for the craft but ensures safety, efficiency, and optimal performance in practical applications. So, how does one keep up with this ever-evolving behemoth? Let's navigate this journey together.

Understanding the Importance of Staying Updated

First, it's crucial to grasp why keeping current is vital. Apart from the obvious reasons like ensuring the best possible care for vehicles, the industry's evolution often dictates safety standards, optimal practices, and introduces tools that can make tasks more manageable and efficient. For DIY car enthusiasts, understanding the latest automotive technologies can mean the difference between a successful repair and potentially costly mistakes.

Subscribing to Relevant Publications

One of the age-old methods of staying informed is subscribing to reputable automotive magazines and journals. **Motor Trend**, **Car and Driver**, and **Automotive News** are some established names in the industry, providing in-depth analyses, reviews, and news on the latest trends and technologies.

But beyond these giants, consider diving into specialized publications tailored to specific car niches, be it electric vehicles, classic cars, or off-road adventures. They often offer detailed insights that mainstream publications might gloss over.

Online Platforms and Communities

The internet has democratized information like never before. Websites, blogs, forums, and social media channels are abundant with automotive content. Platforms like **Jalopnik** or **Autoblog** offer daily updates on automotive news. For those looking for video content, YouTube channels such as **Engineering Explained** break down complex automotive concepts into easily digestible formats.

But remember, with the vastness of the internet, comes the responsibility of discerning reliable sources from the less credible ones. Always cross-check facts and ensure the resource has a good reputation in the community.

Automotive Conventions and Trade Shows

There's reading about technology, and then there's experiencing it firsthand. Automotive trade shows like the **Geneva Motor Show** or **SEMA** in Las Vegas are grand stages where the latest advancements are unveiled. Attending these shows can provide firsthand insights into where the industry is heading and offer opportunities for networking with professionals who share similar interests.

Continuous Learning through Courses and Workshops

Another way to stay ahead is by enrolling in courses or workshops focused on automotive technology. Many institutions and community colleges offer classes on contemporary topics such as hybrid technology, advanced driver-assistance systems (**ADAS**), or electric vehicle maintenance.

Joining Automotive Clubs

Local automotive clubs are more than just venues for showcasing vehicles or sharing a mutual appreciation for cars. They're dynamic communities where members share knowledge, tips, and recent discoveries in the automotive realm. Being part of such a group can provide a regular update on what's new and what's worth noting.

In conclusion, staying updated in the automotive world is an ongoing commitment. It demands proactive engagement, curiosity, and the discernment to separate the signal from the noise. However, the rewards, in terms of knowledge, safety, and the sheer joy of understanding the marvels of modern automotive technology, are well worth the effort. Dive deep, remain curious, and always be willing to learn.

Recommended Reading and Resources: Charting Your Educational Journey

The vast world of automotive knowledge is not confined to a single source or medium. Diverse resources available today can deepen understanding, provide new perspectives, and offer hands-on experience. However, given the deluge of information available, it becomes crucial to find trusted and beneficial materials. Whether you're looking to understand the basics, gain advanced expertise, or just stay updated with the industry's pulse, here's a curated list of resources to guide you further.

Books: Building a Strong Foundation

A well-written book can be an anchor, offering in-depth insights and a structured approach to any subject. When it comes to automotive knowledge, certain books stand out for their clarity, depth, and approachability.

1. **"Zen and the Art of Motorcycle Maintenance" by Robert M. Pirsig**: While not strictly an automotive guide, this classic delves deep into the philosophy of quality in mechanics and life. A compelling read for those who see car repair as both a science and an art.

2. **"The Car Hacker's Handbook" by Craig Smith**: For those keen on the digital side of vehicles, this book explores the computer systems in cars, providing insights into automotive security systems.

3. **"Auto Repair For Dummies" by Deanna Sclar**: A staple for beginners. It demystifies many automotive repair and maintenance tasks in an easy-to-understand format.

4. **"How Cars Work" by Tom Newton**: An illustrative guide detailing the mechanics of cars. Perfect for those who want a visual understanding of automotive systems.

5. **"Drive!: Henry Ford, George Selden, and the Race to Invent the Auto Age" by Lawrence Goldstone**: This book dives into the history of the automobile, providing a rich context to the vehicles we see today.

6. **"The Complete Car Care Manual" by Popular Mechanics**: Covering everything from the basics to more intricate repair tasks, this is a comprehensive guide for any car owner.

Online Forums and Websites: Interactive Learning

The internet has democratized learning, and automotive enthusiasts have a plethora of forums and websites at their disposal. These platforms are great for real-time problem-solving, learning from others' experiences, and keeping up with the latest trends.

1. **CarForums**: As the name suggests, it's a bustling community of car enthusiasts discussing everything from repair tips, reviews, to the latest in automotive technology.

2. **AutomotiveForums**: Another vibrant community where both professionals and hobbyists share knowledge, solve problems, and discuss the latest news.

3. **Pelican Parts Forums**: Especially for European car enthusiasts, this forum provides detailed DIY guides and discussions on models like BMW, Mercedes, and Porsche.

4. **Jalopnik**: A website combining the latest car news with reviews, buyer's guides, and op-eds about the car culture and industry.

5. **MyCarForum**: Offering a platform for car enthusiasts and owners to discuss and share knowledge, news, and updates in the automotive world.

6. **Bob Is The Oil Guy**: A forum that goes in-depth about motor oil and lubrication, giving detailed advice and discussion on everything related to automotive fluids.

Online Courses: Structured and Comprehensive Learning

With the rise of e-learning platforms, you can now get classroom-like experiences from the comfort of your home. These courses range from beginner to advanced levels.

1. **Udemy's "Basic Automotive Maintenance"**: Perfect for those just starting out, this course covers the essentials in bite-sized, easy-to-understand modules.

2. **Coursera's "Introduction to Electric Cars"**: As electric vehicles become mainstream, understanding them is crucial. This course, offered in collaboration with top universities, provides a thorough grounding.

3. **MIT's "Deep Learning for Self-Driving Cars"**: For those looking at the cutting edge of automotive technology, this course dives deep into the AI systems powering autonomous vehicles.

4. **Lynda's "Automotive Engineering"**: An advanced course that goes into the intricate details of car design and production, perfect for those looking to dive deep into the engineering side.

5. **Alison's "Advanced Diploma in Automotive Engineering"**: This course offers a comprehensive understanding of vehicle design, the functionality of various parts, and how to maintain and repair them.

6. **edX's "Principles of Manufacturing" by MITx**: Though not strictly automotive, it covers essential manufacturing processes and techniques that any serious automotive enthusiast would find valuable.

Industry Magazines and Publications

Consistently reading reputable magazines ensures you're updated with trends, reviews, and breakthroughs.

1. **Automotive News**: A comprehensive source of global automotive industry news, analysis, and trending topics.

2. **Motor Trend**: Known for its vehicle reviews and annual car awards.

3. **Road & Track**: Offers both consumer advice and in-depth features on motorsports.

4. **Car and Driver**: An authoritative source for new car reviews, auto show coverage, and expert automotive advice.

5. **Automobile Magazine**: Combining aesthetic tastes with automotive insights, this magazine offers rich articles on design trends, classic cars, and industry movements.

6. **Hemmings Motor News**: Catering especially to classic car enthusiasts, it offers resources on auctions, parts, and vintage events.

In conclusion, the quest for automotive knowledge is a journey, not a destination. As the industry evolves, so should our understanding. By leveraging a mix of books, online platforms, and formal courses, enthusiasts can ensure they're well-equipped to tackle any automotive challenge, whether theoretical or practical, that comes their way.

Automotive Schools and Certification Programs

For many auto enthusiasts, the thrill of working on a car isn't just a hobby—it's a passion. And there's a point where passion pushes us to seek formal knowledge and skills. If you've ever considered transforming this love for vehicles into a full-fledged career or just advancing your skills to a professional level, there are several avenues you can explore. Let's delve into the realm of formal automotive education, from trade schools to certification programs.

Trade Schools: Hands-On Experience

Trade schools, also known as **technical schools**, are institutions specifically designed to impart hands-on skills. These schools provide intensive training programs tailored for individuals who prefer a more practical approach. When enrolled in an automotive trade school, you'll get to work on actual cars, understand their intricate systems, and master the tools and techniques of the trade. It's not just about the theory; it's about getting your hands dirty—literally.

There are several renowned automotive trade schools across the country. Institutions like Universal Technical Institute (UTI) or Lincoln Tech are just a couple of examples. When choosing a trade school, consider factors like the curriculum, the available equipment, and the faculty's expertise.

Community Colleges: A Blend of Theory and Practice

While trade schools emphasize hands-on practice, community colleges offer a balance between theoretical knowledge and practical experience. Many community colleges provide **associate degree programs** in automotive technology. These are usually two-year programs, combining classroom lectures with lab sessions.

Community colleges often have partnerships with local dealerships or automotive businesses, providing students with internship opportunities. This not only allows for real-world experience but also paves the way for job placements after graduation. Moreover, since community colleges are often more affordable than four-year institutions, they present an economical way to gain in-depth automotive knowledge.

Certification Programs: Specialized Skills & Recognition

Once you have a foundational understanding of automotive mechanics, you might want to specialize in certain areas or gain recognition for your expertise. That's where **certification programs** come into play.

The National Institute for Automotive Service Excellence (ASE) is a prominent entity in the U.S. that offers certification in various automotive specialties—from repair and maintenance to advanced diagnostics. Being ASE-certified is not just a testament to your skills; it's a badge of trustworthiness in the automotive industry.

To get certified, you'll need to pass the ASE test and have relevant work experience. The certification is valid for five years, after which you'd need to renew it, ensuring that certified professionals stay updated with the ever-evolving automotive technologies.

Making the Right Choice

Choosing between trade schools, community colleges, and certification programs depends on your goals. If you're aiming for a quick entry into the job market with hands-on skills, trade schools might be your best bet. If you're looking for a balanced approach with both theoretical and practical insights, community colleges are ideal. And if you already have some experience and aim for specialization or industry recognition, consider certification programs.

Remember, while formal education can provide structured knowledge and open doors to professional opportunities, continuous learning is key in the automotive world. Technology is ever-evolving, and as auto enthusiasts or professionals, we must evolve with it. Whether you opt for a school, college, or certification program, always keep that spark of curiosity alive. It's this passion and thirst for knowledge that drives the automotive world forward.

Appendix

By familiarizing yourself with these terms, you'll be better equipped to understand your car's mechanics, making conversations with mechanics or fellow car enthusiasts more enlightening. Remember, knowledge is power, especially when it comes to vehicle maintenance and operation.

1. **ABS (Anti-lock Braking System)**: A system that stops brakes from locking up and skidding, ensuring that the wheels keep turning and maintaining the driver's control over the vehicle.

2. **Aftermarket**: Parts made by someone other than the vehicle manufacturer. They're like getting an accessory for your phone from a third-party store, not the phone's brand.

3. **Air Filter**: A part that cleans the air going into the engine. It acts like our noses filtering the air we breathe.

4. **Alternator**: A generator that converts mechanical energy into electrical energy, powering your car's electrical system and charging the battery.

5. **Ball Joint**: A pivot point that allows the suspension to move and rotate.

6. **Battery**: Stores electricity to start the car and power any electrical parts.

7. **Brake Fluid**: A type of hydraulic fluid used in brake systems to help apply the pressure needed to stop the vehicle.

8. **Brake Pads**: Materials that create friction against the brake rotors, helping to stop the car.

9. **Camshaft**: A rotating shaft inside the engine that opens and closes the intake and exhaust valves.

10. **Carburetor**: Mixes air with fuel for older internal combustion engines.

11. **Catalytic Converter**: A device in the exhaust system that reduces the toxicity of emissions from an internal combustion engine.

12. **Chassis**: The base frame of a vehicle, akin to the skeleton in our body.

13. **Clutch**: Engages and disengages power transmission, especially from the driving shaft to the driven shaft.

14. **Combustion Chamber**: Where the magic happens in an engine: fuel, air, and spark combine to produce combustion, which moves the pistons.

15. **Crankshaft**: Converts the up-and-down motion of the engine's pistons into a rotational movement that turns the vehicle's wheels.

16. **CV Joint (Constant Velocity Joint)**: Allows the drive shaft to transmit power through a variable angle, at a constant rotational speed, without an appreciable increase in friction.

17. **Differential**: A device that divides the engine's torque two ways, allowing each output to spin at a different speed.

18. **Distributor**: Distributes high voltage from the ignition coil to the spark plugs in the correct firing order.

19. **Drive Belt**: A belt that drives things like the alternator, power steering pump, and air-conditioning compressor.

20. **Drive Shaft**: Connects the transmission to the differential, transferring rotation and power to the vehicle's axles.

21. **EGR Valve (Exhaust Gas Recirculation Valve)**: Part of the emissions system that reintroduces a portion of the exhaust gases back into the engine for burning again.

22. **Engine Control Unit (ECU)**: The car's brain, overseeing a variety of functions.

23. **Exhaust Manifold**: Channels the exhaust gases from multiple cylinders into one pipe.

24. **Flywheel**: Stores rotational energy. In manual cars, it assists in transferring engine power to the drivetrain.

25. **Fuel Injector**: A valve that sprays fuel into an engine's combustion chambers at precise times.

26. **Fuel Pump**: Draws fuel from the tank and pumps it to the engine.

27. **Gasket**: A seal, usually made of thin material, that ensures a tight seal between two metal parts, preventing leaks.

28. **Gearbox (Transmission)**: Adjusts the level of power available to a car's wheels.

29. **Hybrid**: Vehicles that combine traditional combustion engines with electric motors to enhance efficiency.

30. **Intake Manifold**: A series of tubes that distribute the air coming into the engine evenly to each of the cylinders.

31. **Jump Start**: Using another vehicle's battery or another external power source to start a vehicle when its battery is exhausted.

32. **Knocking**: A rattling noise you hear when the air-fuel mixture in the cylinders is detonating in more than once place at a time.

33. **Lug Nuts**: The nuts that hold the wheels on the vehicle.

34. **Master Cylinder**: A key component of the brake hydraulic system that stores the brake fluid.

35. **Muffler**: Reduces the noise produced by the engine's exhaust gases.

36. **Neutral**: A gear that disconnects the engine from the wheels so the engine can run without making the car move.

37. **OBD (On-Board Diagnostics)**: A vehicle's self-diagnosing and reporting capability, which gives the vehicle owner or a repair technician access to the status of various vehicle subsystems.

38. **Oil Filter**: Filters out contaminants, ensuring that the oil remains clean as it circulates through an engine.

39. **Oil Pan**: Holds the oil required for the system in a reservoir.

40. **Powertrain**: Refers to the main components that generate power and deliver it to the wheels.

41. **Radiator**: Helps to keep the engine cool by circulating coolant through the engine and releasing the heat into the air.

42. **Rotor (or Disc)**: A component of disc brakes – it's what the brake pads squeeze onto to stop the wheels from turning.

43. **Shock Absorbers**: Help to dampen the movement of the suspension and keep the tires on the road, ensuring a smooth ride.

44. **Spark Plug**: Provides the spark needed for the explosion in the combustion chamber.

45. **Struts**: These are structural elements of your car's suspension, helping to keep your ride smooth.

46. **Suspension**: This is the system in your car that supports its weight, absorbs bumps, and helps it handle better when turning or navigating rough terrain. Think of it as a bridge between your car and the road.

47. **Throttle**: It's like your car's "accelerator pedal". When you step on the gas, the throttle controls how much air flows into the engine, determining how fast you go.

48. **Timing Belt**: This keeps the engine's camshaft and crankshaft turning at synchronized rates. It's like a conductor ensuring all musicians in an orchestra play in time.

49. **Torque**: Refers to the turning force of your engine. Imagine it as the muscle behind your car's speed, pushing you forward or allowing you to climb hills.

50. **Transmission Fluid**: This liquid helps keep the gears in your gearbox moving smoothly, a bit like how oil lubricates the engine.

51. **Tread**: The patterned part of your tire that touches the road. It provides grip, especially in conditions like rain or snow.

52. **Turbocharger**: A device that pushes more air into the combustion chamber, allowing the engine to burn more fuel and, in turn, produce more power. Think of it as a "boost" button for your car's engine.

53. **Valve**: These control the flow of liquids and gases in and out of the engine. Picture them as doors that open and close at specific times during the engine cycle.

54. **VIN (Vehicle Identification Number)**: This is your car's unique "fingerprint". It's a series of numbers and letters specific to each vehicle, revealing details about its make, model, and history.

55. **Viscosity**: A term that describes how thick or thin a liquid is. In cars, it's often used to talk about the thickness of oils and how well they flow.

56. **Water Pump**: Circulates coolant throughout the engine and radiator to keep the engine at the right temperature, much like how our heart circulates blood to regulate body temperature.

57. **Wheelbase**: The distance between the front and rear axles of your car. It can influence things like how smooth the ride is and how easily the car turns.

58. **Yaw**: Refers to the side-to-side movement of the car, especially when turning. If you've ever felt your car swing wide in a fast turn, that's yaw in action.

59. **Zerk Fitting**: A small fitting on a machine or vehicle where grease is pumped in to lubricate moving parts. It's like a doorway for a special type of oil to keep things moving smoothly.

60. **Zero Emissions**: Refers to vehicles or machines that release no pollutants into the atmosphere when they operate. Think of it as an environmentally-friendly stamp of approval, often associated with electric vehicles.

61. **Zone Heating**: This system allows different areas (or "zones") inside your car to have different temperature settings. If you've ever wanted your side warmer than the passenger's side, you've used zone heating.

Useful Conversion Charts

In the realm of automotive work, one of the challenges that both professionals and enthusiasts often face is the diversity of measurement systems. Depending on the origin of the vehicle or the part, you might encounter specifications in the metric system, the imperial system, or sometimes both. Given that precision is paramount in this field, having a clear understanding and quick reference to convert between these units can be immensely useful. That's where **conversion charts** come into play.

Understanding why there are different measurement systems can be rooted back to history and regional preferences. For instance, while most of the world now operates on the metric system, countries like the United States predominantly use the imperial system. This duality is evident in the automotive world, where an American car might measure tire pressure in psi, but a European model would use bar or kPa.

Why Conversion Charts Matter

Imagine you're working on a classic American car but using a toolset you bought overseas. Your tools might be in millimeters, but the specifications for the car could be in inches. Without accurate conversion, you risk using the wrong tool or setting, which can lead to damaging the part or obtaining an inaccurate result.

Moreover, for those who engage in international automotive activities, like buying parts online from different countries, understanding these conversions ensures you're getting the right component for your vehicle.

Handy Reference Conversions

1. **Length**

   - **Inches to Millimeters**: Multiply the length value by 25.4.

     - *Example: 5 inches is 5 x 25.4 = 127 millimeters.*

   - **Millimeters to Inches**: Divide the length value by 25.4.

     - *Example: 50 millimeters is 50 ÷ 25.4 ≈ 1.97 inches.*

2. **Volume**

   - **Gallons to Liters**: Multiply the volume value by 3.785.

- *Example: 5 gallons is 5 x 3.785 = 18.925 liters.*

- **Liters to Gallons**: Divide the volume value by 3.785.

  - *Example: 20 liters is 20 ÷ 3.785 ≈ 5.28 gallons.*

3. **Pressure**

   - **PSI to kPa**: Multiply the pressure value by 6.895.

     - *Example: 30 psi is 30 x 6.895 = 206.85 kPa.*

   - **kPa to PSI**: Divide the pressure value by 6.895.

     - *Example: 100 kPa is 100 ÷ 6.895 ≈ 14.5 psi.*

4. **Temperature** (less common in auto work but still useful)

   - **Fahrenheit to Celsius**: Subtract 32, then multiply by 5/9.

     - *Example: 68°F is (68 - 32) x 5/9 = 20°C.*

   - **Celsius to Fahrenheit**: Multiply by 9/5, then add 32.

     - *Example: 20°C is 20 x 9/5 + 32 = 68°F.*

Keep in mind that while these conversions offer a practical way to switch between units, always ensure you're rounding appropriately, especially when precision is crucial.

A Tip for the Digital Age

In this digital era, there are various apps and online calculators designed specifically for unit conversion. While our reference guide provides a manual method, don't hesitate to leverage technology for quicker conversions, especially for complex calculations. However, it's always beneficial to understand the underlying math, as it gives a foundation that tech tools build upon.

In conclusion, while the presence of multiple measurement systems might seem confusing at first, with the right tools and knowledge, navigating between them becomes second nature. Always remember the importance of accuracy in automotive work and ensure your conversions are precise to guarantee optimal outcomes. As you dive deeper into your automotive journey, these conversion charts and the understanding behind them will undoubtedly serve as invaluable companions.

Dear Reader,

Thank you for purchasing my book. I am deeply grateful for your support and interest. If you enjoyed the content, I would appreciate it if you could leave a review. Your feedback is very valuable to me.

Thank you!!!

Printed in Great Britain
by Amazon

44468486R00090